UPHOLDING *the* RULE OF LAW

IN THE SOCIAL SECURITY ADMINISTRATION, AN AGENCY AT WAR WITH ITSELF

JUDGE FRANK B BOROWIEC

[signature]

iUniverse, Inc.
Bloomington

Atlanta, Ga 5/12/17

Upholding the Rule of Law
in the Social Security Administration, an Agency at War with Itself

iUniverse books may be ordered through booksellers or by contacting:

iUniverse
1663 Liberty Drive
Bloomington, IN 47403
www.iuniverse.com
1-800-Authors (1-800-288-4677)

ISBN: 978-1-4502-7362-6 (sc)
ISBN: 978-1-4502-7363-3 (dj)
ISBN: 978-1-4502-7364-0 (ebk)

Library of Congress Control Number: 2010917402

Printed in the United States of America

iUniverse rev. date: 01/07/2011

August 1986
Be it resolved, That The

American Bar Association
Hereby Commends, The

Social Security Administrative Law Judge Corps
For Its Outstanding Efforts During
The Period From 1982–1984 To Protect The
Integrity Of Administrative Adjudication
Within Their Agency, To Preserve The Public's
Confidence In The Fairness Of Governmental
Institutions, And To Uphold The Rule Of Law

This citation was awarded to me and my fellow judges at the American Bar Association's annual dinner in Lincoln Center, New York City, on the night of August 11, 1986. As far as I know, such an award by the American Bar Association to single out and commend a specific group of administrative law judges is without precedent.

It is proudly displayed on the wall of my study. The following story chronicles those events in my life that led to this award.

PREFACE

―

"Everything is determined, the beginning as well as the end, by forces over which we have no control. It is determined for the insect, as well as the star. Human beings, vegetables, or cosmic dust, we all dance to a mysterious tune, intoned in the distance by an invisible piper."
—Albert Einstein

In my life, a series of seemingly unrelated events ultimately led me to be a member of that small group of judges recognized by the American Bar Association for upholding the rule of law.

This led to me to question the writings of William Shakespeare, who penned in his play *Julius Caesar*, "The fault, dear Brutus, is not in our stars, but in ourselves ..." and to adopt the conclusions of Friedrich Wilhelm Nietzsche in *Human, All Too Human*, who believed that "our destiny exercises its influence over us even when, as yet, we have not learned its nature."

The inclusion in this book of my education, military experiences, and early law practice exemplifies the importance of certain significant and insignificant events that directed my life and career in directions that I had never envisioned.

To illustrate, World War II was most certainly a significant event. At its onset I was at the University of Buffalo pursuing my childhood dream to become an engineer. The three years of military service that intervened were significant in that I decided in that time frame that I did not want to be an engineer, but would you believe, I wanted to pursue a career in the law. The GI Bill made that career goal attainable.

So I have incorporated my earlier life experiences in this book, to identify that early part of my student, military, and legal experiences that led to an award from the American Bar Association for upholding the rule of law and to honor and acknowledge the importance of those mentors in the formative periods of my life that so dramatically influenced my future. Their inclusion also allows the reader to recognize that whatever personal goals I might have achieved would not have been possible without their wisdom and direction.

The raison d'être for this book, of course, has to be the recognition of the classic conflict between government agencies' need to efficiently and effectively execute and fulfill their statutory mandates and the administrative law judges' sworn duty as independent, unbiased, and impartial arbiters to protect the due process interests of individuals and to ensure a fair hearing free of agency influence. This book attempts to identify and document a number of small battles in that inevitable war and the need for eternal vigilance to identify and combat any agency encroachment on their position and status under the Administrative Procedure Act.

Our responsibilities as administrative law judges was most succinctly and beautifully defined by Sir Derek Oulton, permanent secretary to the Lord Chancellor and clerk to the Crown in Chancery, who spoke at a meeting we had with our British counterparts in London, England. In Britain, the independence and integrity of the administrative law judges is a matter of such importance that their direct superior is the Lord High Chancellor.

Sir Derek noted our common antecedents with the tribunes of ancient Rome who stood between the autocratic patricians and the plebeians just as administrative law judges now protect the rights of individuals contesting autocratic government actions. Sir Derek used poetry eloquently and elegantly when he quoted from T. B. Macaulay's *Lays of Ancient Rome* to illustrate the historical similarity between the British and American administrative law judges and the ancient Roman tribunes.

> *For then there was no Tribune to speak*
> *The word of might.*
> *Which make the rich man tremble,*
> *and guards the poor man's right.*

MY BEGINNINGS

I have always regretted that, in spite of all of the opportunities to do so, I never really explored with my grandparents what their lives were like as children and young adults. My maternal grandfather was Frank X. Boroszewski, who I know was born on November 17, 1870, immigrated to the United States, and became a very successful businessman. At age twenty-four, he married Martha Szulc, and they had seven children who became church organists, teachers, doctors, and attorneys. That limited knowledge was really all that I knew of his life, other than that he was a kind, generous, and caring grandparent.

Years after his death in 1955, in trying to discover where and when he arrived in this country, I came upon a passenger list from the Port of New York dated December 21, 1886, documenting the arrival of a sixteen-year-old male, Franz Boraszewsky, on the steamer *California*, which had departed Europe from the Port of Hamburg, Germany. It disclosed that the *California* had been built in Glasgow, Scotland, in 1872 and was powered by a single screw engine and three masts.

A hundred questions popped up in my mind. My grandfather had just turned sixteen a month before he sailed, so how did he get the funds to purchase his ticket for a transatlantic voyage? How did he get to Hamburg, Germany, from his home in Poland? What was the sea voyage like? Where did he spend Christmas Day? How did he pay for his travel from the Port of New York to Buffalo, New York? How did he select Buffalo as his final destination? What did his parents have to say about all of this? A hundred questions and no answers!

I was born on December 26, 1924, in Buffalo, New York, the eldest child of Frances (née Boroszewska) and Chester Borowiec. I had two brothers, Mitchel and Richard, and a sister, Delphine. My early education was at the St. Florian and Transfiguration elementary schools and East High School.

I was a senior at East High School on December 7, 1941, when the Empire of Japan attacked Pearl Harbor. Nineteen days later I turned eighteen and became eligible for the draft. After graduation from East High School in June of 1942, I became a member of the freshman engineering class at the University of Buffalo.

Prior to graduation from high school, while working as a stagehand for the senior play, one of my classmates in a casual conversation mentioned that in the morning newspaper[1] there was an announcement that the US Army Air Corps was recruiting a limited number of students for a meteorological program that was to begin in January of 1943. Interested parties were advised to submit an application, and if initially qualified, final selection would be based on the results of a written examination. I applied and was duly notified to be at the Buffalo Science Museum auditorium, where the examination would take place in July of 1942.

I appeared bright and early, and much to my surprise and disappointment, the auditorium was filled to capacity with students hoping to qualify for the program. The sheer size of the crowd made

---

1   *Buffalo Courier Express*, May 1942.

me realize that my chances of success were somewhere between zero and nil.

I began my university studies and quickly forgot about the meteorological program. My classes and my 1-A draft status were occupying all my attention when, lo and behold, I received a letter dated January 19, 1943, from the War Department[2] that I had been selected for their program. I was ordered to report to my local Draft Board # 601 and request immediate induction, which I was most happy to do. The good Lord must have been looking after me, as I was the only person in that auditorium selected for the program.

---

2   War Department Letter, Headquarters Army Air Forces, January 19, 1943.

THE WAR YEARS

~

January 30, 1943–February 19, 1946

On the thirtieth day of January 1943, my dad drove me to the army induction center in the Ellicott Square Building in downtown Buffalo for my physical. There I was formally inducted into the US Army Air Corps.

When I first told my mother and dad that I planned to enlist in the army, rather than be drafted, they were horrified. When I explained that I had to enlist in order to become a student at Hamilton College for two years, they were overjoyed.

By three in the afternoon, I had passed my physical exam, and I and twenty-three others were duly sworn in as members of the US Armed Forces at 5:35 p.m. I was assigned a serial number, which would have to be engraved on all of my earthly possessions for the next three years.

At six in the evening, we left for Fort Niagara, and arrived there at 10:00 p.m. My new mailing address was

Company F
1213 C.C.
Fort Niagara, New York

On Monday, February 1, in a cafeteria-like setting, I was given two large duffle bags in which I tossed my new GI jacket, shirts, socks, shoes, and so on. Surprisingly, they all fit remarkably well.

I was then given an IQ test. I scored 130. On the second and third of February, our company spent the days drilling, drilling, and more drilling.

On the afternoon of the fourth of February, I was told to pack up, as I was shipping out. No mention was made of a destination. A bus carried us to the train station in Niagara Falls, and I boarded a darkened day coach with my fellow recruits. We traveled nonstop, passing through Buffalo, New York; Philadelphia, Pennsylvania; and Camden, New Jersey, arriving in Atlantic City, New Jersey, the next day at one fifteen in the afternoon.

We were met at the train by Sergeant Fredienburg and were taken by bus to the Claridge Hotel. Incredibly, I would do my army basic training on the boardwalks of Atlantic City, New Jersey, marching to the accompaniment of the Glenn Miller Orchestra.

ATLANTIC CITY, NEW JERSEY

February 1943

The Claridge Hotel had been taken over by the army, and its original plush furniture had been replaced with two double-decked cots and four footlockers, in which we placed our belongings. Yet we had our own bath, a real luxury compared to the usual army barracks.

My new mailing address was
920th Squadron Group
Flight D
Claridge Hotel, Room 106
Atlantic City, New Jersey

That afternoon, we were assigned to our individual companies, and of course, a drill sergeant. The next morning, we raggedly marched to our training site. We quickly mastered the basic marching maneuvers, and by day's end we smartly marched and sang our way back to our hotel, where we were greeted by the Glenn Miller Orchestra.

Nighttime in Atlantic City quickly brought us back to the reality that was World War II. German submarines that could be silhouetted against the New Jersey coastline lay off the coast, waiting to attack an unwary ship. For that reason, a total blackout was imposed along the coast after dusk. Still, it was not unusual to look out to sea and see the bright flames emanating from a ship that had been torpedoed.

Four weeks of marching, singing, and drilling came to an abrupt end on March 1, 1943. My orders came through. I was shipping out at 1:00 p.m. Our group arrived in New York City at 5:15 p.m., ate dinner in Grand Central Station, and then marched to our train in Grand Central Station singing the Army Air Corps song. Oh happy day!

We arrived in Utica, New York, at 1:00 a.m.; arrived in Clinton, New York, at 1:30 a.m.; arrived at Hamilton College at 2:00 a.m.; and made it to bed at 3:00 a.m.

Reveille was at 6:15 a.m., and one class was scheduled in the morning. I, of course, slept all afternoon, and after dinner was back in bed by 9:00 p.m.

My new address was
> United States Army Air Forces
> Technical Training Detachment No. 18
> Flight 8, Room 27, South Dorm
> Hamilton, College, Clinton, New York

HAMILTON COLLEGE

—

1943–1944

Hamilton College was founded in 1793 and is a private, independent liberal arts college located in Clinton, New York. The college is named for Alexander Hamilton, who was a member of the first board of trustees, though he never set foot on campus. Hamilton is sometimes referred to as the College on the Hill because of the school's location on top of College Hill, just outside of downtown Clinton. Hamilton College is one of the "Little Ivies."

In 1943 Hamilton was an all-male school. (It did not become coeducational until 1978.) In the year that had elapsed since Pearl Harbor, the draft had decimated the student population, and prospects for its survival were bleak. To save Hamilton and other similarly situated colleges, the War Department had entered into agreements with these schools to use their expertise to train soldiers in needed military specialties in medicine, science, and administration.

In 1943 there were only sixty-five civilian students on the campus. The student body was almost totally military, that is, two hundred cadets divided into eight flights of twenty-five men housed in the North and South Dorms. I was assigned to flight eight.

Our daily routine never changed. Our first formation was in the quadrangle at 6:30 a.m., followed by breakfast at 7:00 a.m. Classes began at 8:00 a.m. and continued through 9:30 p.m., thankfully with appropriate breaks for lunch and dinner. Initially, all meals were served on dishes instead of scooped-out trays. The mere raising of a hand would send a woman dashing madly between the tables to get us anything and everything, from a second helping of pie to an additional napkin. Emptied dishes were left standing, to be taken away, washed, and made ready for the next meal. We ate heartily and grew fat. Then a strong dose of reality hit. We were issued GI mess kits and steel trays, which were to be used at all future meals.

The class schedule was rigorous, and all classes were taught by the Hamilton faculty, whose reputations in scholarship were impeccable. In any given semester, we took classes in geology, calculus, and various math and science courses to prepare us to be meteorologists. These engineering courses proved to be invaluable. As an engineer, I was taught that you are required to use your analytical skills to recognize and define a problem and then use your knowledge and experience to find a suitable solution to that problem.

The difficult subject matter inherent in these classes took a heavy toll on the student body; over the course of our stay at Hamilton College, approximately 20 percent flunked out.

These valuable credit hours quickly piled up, and when I applied for admission to law school after World War II ended, they expedited my admission to the University of Buffalo School of Law. My only regret was that so few of my credit hours reflected courses in literature, history, English, or philosophy.

In the spring of 1944, we were notified that the US Army Air Force had a surplus of meteorologists, and our program was canceled. We were given a choice. Option A was to enter into a similar program at the University of Virginia to train as administrators to govern conquered territories in postwar Europe; option B was to return to active duty at a weather office at an army airfield.

We were not aware, nor could we be so prescient to foresee that whatever option we chose would have ominous consequences!

For me, the decision was an easy one. I was tired of "college life," and I was not particularly interested in training to be an administrator.

Most of my fellow students chose option A and the good life at the University of Virginia.

I was quickly assigned to the air base at Fort Worth, Texas, where I reported for duty in March of 1944.

For those students who chose the University of Virginia and the Army Specialized Training Program ... horror of horrors ... two months after they began their classes, the program was canceled, and all of the students were transferred to an Infantry Replacement Company in Mississippi to serve as needed rifleman replacements for GIs killed or wounded in combat in the European theater of operations. After a short training period, they were sent to battle. In V-mails they sent to me in Texas, they would report the names of my comrades who had died or been wounded by enemy fire.

The Army Specialized Training Program trained more than two hundred thousand soldiers at 227 colleges in foreign languages, medicine, engineering, and other critical fields needed by the military. On February 18, 1944, the program was discontinued, and the students were assigned to infantry, airborne, and armored divisions.

TEXAS

1944

Arriving at the Fort Worth Army Airfield was a profound experience after almost a year on the quiet, idyllic, and bucolic atmosphere of the Hamilton College campus. Upon getting off the bus at the airfield, I was greeted by the roar of a squadron of B-24 Liberator bombers preparing for takeoff. The earsplitting din from their engines literally shook your body. Tarrant Field was the major staging area for bomber crews who would soon be flying missions in the South Pacific. This earsplitting sound was repeated every morning as the squadrons departed on their training flights.

I quickly entered into training as a weather observer, work which mainly consisted of entering data on weather maps received by teletype from weather stations throughout the country. In addition, we secured temperature, barometric pressure, dew point, and winds aloft readings at our weather station for transmittal.

I was walking to the mess hall on June 6, 1944, when every loudspeaker on the base came on, carrying the voice of General Dwight Eisenhower announcing that American and British troops had launched the long-expected invasion of Europe. Being on the air base on that date and at that time when the outcome of that endeavor was still in doubt made me feel I was a part of history!

Once I had become proficient in executing my duties as a weather observer, I was promoted to corporal. Hurrah.

With the promotion came a transfer and my first air flight in an AT-6 aircraft to Foster Field, Texas. I still remember the excitement of seeing the ground drop away from our plane as we flew from Fort Worth to Matagorda Island, where Foster Field was operational. Foster Field was a flying school for new pilots, and the AT-6 dual seater was especially well suited for that purpose. Entry or departure from Matagorda Island is possible only by plane or by ship out of Port O'Connor, Texas.

Matagorda Island is located in the Gulf of Mexico and in 1944 was used not only as a flight school but also as a gunnery range for fighter aircraft. I was stuck at Foster Field for the foreseeable future, where the only activities after active duty hours were leather craft, bowling, swimming, and a movie. The prospect of being stranded on this sandy backwater for the duration of World War II was unthinkable. There was a war going on, and I wanted to be a part of it. I requested an overseas assignment in an active combat zone. My request was granted, and I was off to fight the war in the South Pacific.

THE SOUTH PACIFIC THEATER
OF OPERATIONS

~

New Guinea, Manila, and Okinawa

M y deployment orders allowed me a furlough, which I spent with my family in Buffalo, New York. Then I went by rail to Provo, Utah, which served as an assembly point for all of us destined for overseas duty. Once assembled, we left by train for San Francisco, and on April 26, 1945, I boarded a troop ship, the USS *Robin Doncaster*.

The first three days out of San Francisco were not very pleasant. We soon discovered that the Pacific Ocean is not very pacific off the coast of California. There seemed to an awful lot of activity around the ship's guardrails. Luckily, after three days out it was smooth sailing.

We played a lot of cards on deck and routinely did our PT exercises to maintain our physical fitness. There were about eight hundred of us on board, so we were limited to two meals a day, breakfast and dinner. As you can imagine, the chow lines were endless.

For five days, our ship glided swiftly through the ocean waters. One thousand miles from the coast of California, halfway to Pearl Harbor,

Hawaii, disaster struck. Somehow, salty ocean water had infiltrated the ship's engines, and we suddenly resembled a vessel trapped and entombed on a windless sea. Samuel Taylor Coleridge in the "The Rime of the Ancient Mariner" colorfully described our plight.

> Day after day, day after day,
>   We stuck, nor breath nor motion;
> As idle as a painted ship
>   Upon a painted ocean.

> Water, water, everywhere,
>   And all the boards did shrink;
> Water, water, everywhere,
>   Nor any drop to drink.

> Alone, alone, all, all alone,
> Alone on a wide wide sea!

Our situation was much more serious in that there were reports of Japanese submarines operating in the area. The *Robin Doncaster*, however, did have a five-inch gun manned by a small navy crew assigned to our ship.

There, of course, was a total blackout, and after dark the gun crews were constantly on the ready. That first night, the gun crew observed some type of suspicious activity off the ship's stern, and the stillness of the night was broken by the loud clangs of a five-inch shell being inserted into the gun's breech, a sound that reverberated throughout the ship. It turned out that some playful dolphins were the cause of the gun crew's alarm. I can guarantee that after that episode, no one slept below decks.

We had floated aimlessly for five days, when suddenly, an American destroyer appeared on the horizon, drew near, threw us a line, and towed us into Pearl Harbor on May 12, 1945.

We entered Pearl Harbor a little more than three years after the Japanese attack, but the sunken battleships were a vivid reminder of the damage inflicted.

We were taken to Camp Aiea, which was located in the city of Honolulu, and for fifteen days I vacationed in Hawaii. A "Circle Tour" of the island of Oahu enabled me to visit Diamond Head, see the amazing black sand beaches, travel up to the Nuuanu Pali Lookout, and shop in Honolulu. It was hard to believe that there still was a war going on.

On May 22, 1945, the repairs to the ship were complete, and we left the Hawaiian Islands. Three days out we were told that the city of Manila in the Philippine Islands had been captured by American forces, and this was now our destination. Eighteen days later, on June 10, 1945, we disembarked.

We were bused to Clark Air Base, a short distance from Manila, for processing. En route, the detritus of the battle for Manila was readily visible—craters, where mortar shells had exploded, interspersed with foxholes used by the defenders of the city and the occasional corpse of a Japanese soldier that had not yet been buried.

My orders were on hand at the processing center, and on June 18, 1945, I was assigned to the Forty-Sixth Air Force Weather Station, APO 713-1 of the Fifteenth Weather Squadron, at Nadzab, New Guinea. *Where in the world*, I wondered, *is Nadzab, New Guinea?*

NADZAB, NEW GUINEA

It is about one thousand miles from Manila to Nadzab. Our C-47 noisily covered the distance, making refueling stops at the islands of Moratai and Biak. There was no airfield at Nadzab, so we landed at the coastal city of Lae and then took a long jeep ride into the interior of New Guinea to my new home in Nadzab.

The New Guinea campaign began on January 24, 1943, and officially ended on December 31, 1944, six months prior to my arrival. There still were isolated pockets of Japanese in the jungle, but they were not regarded as a significant threat. As we drove through the jungle in our jeep from Lae to Nadzab, that assurance was not very comforting. Thankfully, we arrived safely at my new weather station.

The military campaign on New Guinea is now all but forgotten, except by those who served there. Battles with names like Tarawa, Saipan, and Iwo Jima overshadowed it. In total, the New Guinea campaign resulted in 33,500 casualties, and about 70 percent were Australian. The Japanese had transformed Lae into a major air base and a well-fortified anchorage, so an amphibious invasion was not feasible because of the lack of sufficient landing craft and barges.

New Guinea is the second-largest island in the world just south of the equator. The Owen Stanley mountain range cuts across the center of the entire island. That, coupled with the lush interior tropical jungle that swallowed men and equipment, made any overland passage or movement of troops virtually impossible. Malaria, dengue fever, dysentery, scrub typhus, and a plethora of other tropical sicknesses awaited unwary soldiers in the jungle. As a result, all settlements and army bases had to be located along the coastline.

The Allied armies needed to capture Lae because of its strategic position as a major staging area for the Japanese armies. The Australians and American troops began a pincer movement along the coast to isolate and capture this stronghold. In such rugged jungle terrain, a few determined men could slow down a division, and the numerous streams cut the coastline into a swampy, muddy bog. Casualties were heavy.

A new approach was needed. Air reconnaissance revealed that about twenty miles west of Nadzab was a large, grassy mountainous plateau that was well suited for a parachute assault. On September 5, 1945, unchallenged by Japanese air power, ninety-six C-47 transports, escorted by two hundred fighters and bombers, ferried an infantry regiment to the Nadzab plain. The Japanese were caught by surprise, and hundreds of American paratroopers emptied out of the C-47s in five minutes. They quickly secured the landing zone, and the C-47s then began to fly in the Australian Seventh Division to the airhead. The Japanese Eighteenth Army was outflanked and was forced to leave Lae. The luckless Japanese had to detour around the Australians blocking the coastal road and march into the rugged twelve-thousand-foot mountains to escape capture. Eight thousand officers and men trekked into the foreboding mountains. More than two thousand Japanese never came out of the mountains; most were the victims of starvation.

I had apparently traded the sandy backwater of Matagorda Island, Texas, for the backwater of Nadzab, New Guinea. Incidentally, I never saw anything that resembled a city, town, or hamlet in the area. The most exciting event was a large earthquake that shook the very ground where I was standing. My first thought when hearing the roaring noise was that it emanated from a convoy of army trucks, but there were no trucks in the area.

By the summer of 1945, while I was languishing in the jungles of New Guinea, the war against the Japanese had speeded up both in scope and intensity. The battle for the Philippines had ended with the capture of Manila on March 3, 1945, after a bitter thirty-day struggle. The Iwo Jima invasion had taken place on February 19, 1945, and American forces had landed on Okinawa on April 1, 1945. The war in Europe ended on May 8, 1945. In New Guinea the most significant event was the capture of the village of Numoikum on August 8, 1945, by troops of the Sixth Australian Division.

Luckily, my tour of duty at Nadzab came to an end when the air force decided that it did not require a weather station at Nadzab, and I was reassigned to a weather station on the island of Okinawa.

OKINAWA

T he weather station was located at the Motobu Air Strip, which had been captured by the Sixth Marine Division on April 20, 1945. The island of Okinawa was deemed secure on June 21, 1945. The price of victory was high. Japanese dead totaled one hundred eight thousand. The army and navy incurred total casualties of forty-two thousand. These figures were very sobering in that they portended the large casualty losses that would be incurred in the invasion of Japan by one million GIs.

The United States, however, had secretly developed an atomic bomb, and its introduction into the conflict had dramatic results. On July 28, 1945, the United States, Great Britain, and China called on Japan to surrender unconditionally or face "prompt and utter destruction." The proclamation was signed by President Harry Truman, Prime Minister Winston Churchill, and Generalissimo Chiang Kai-Shek. Absent an affirmative reply, the first atomic bomb was dropped August 6, 1945, on Hiroshima, and a second on Nagasaki on August 9, 1945.

In the span of nine days, two atomic bombs fell, the Soviet Union declared war on Japan, and Japan sued for peace.

Allied warships, protected by fighters and bombers, began to enter Tokyo Bay on August 28, 1945. The formal surrender would be signed aboard the battleship *Missouri* on September 2, 1945.

The imminent signing of the peace treaty produced a flurry of activity, as an army of occupation had to be transported, primarily by air, to the Japanese islands.

Within days, orders were issued, and I was reassigned to be a member of a small complement of weather and tower (air traffic control) personnel to activate the operational status of the Yokota Air Field in Irumagawa, Japan, which is a suburb of the Japanese capital, Tokyo. Until we arrived and took over these duties and made the airfield operational, no troop airships could be safely landed.

The flight into Japan was, to say the least, quite scary. For the first time, we were flying into an air base that had not been secured by the army, navy, or marines. Did the Japanese soldiers at the airfield know that the war was over? Would we encounter some dedicated individuals who had not gotten the word of war's end? Would the pilot of our aircraft be able to successfully initiate a landing at the airfield? Lots of questions and no answers.

I had been chasing the war ever since I volunteered in January of 1943. After a tour as a meteorology student and assignments to very comfortable backwaters in Texas, New Guinea, and Okinawa, when I finally caught up with the war in 1945, it was over.

JAPAN

I n spite of our fears, we landed safely at the Yokota Air Base. We were warmly greeted by Mr. Yuseke Nahasage, the Japanese weatherman on duty at the airfield. This was incredible. We really did not expect a warm welcome from the Japanese because of the bitterness and ferocity of the battles that had taken place since Pearl Harbor. Yet, once their Emperor Hirohito had announced that all hostilities were over and a new era of peace was beginning, his loyal subjects dutifully obeyed. Thanks be to God.

The Yokota Air Base was located in the city of Irumagawa, Japan, a few miles outside of Tokyo, and happily as it turned out, on the main subway line to Tokyo itself. This airfield was known by the Japanese as the Irumagawa Air Field; I knew it as the Yokota Air Force Base. It was later renamed the Johnson Air Force Base in honor of its commanding officer, Gerald A. Johnson, a fighter pilot who scored twenty-two victories but was killed postwar when his B-25 crashed over Tokyo Bay.

I was promoted to sergeant. My new address was
    Yokota Air Force Base, 20th Weather Squadron
    111th Army Air Force Weather Station
    APO 704
    San Francisco, California

Tokyo was the big attraction, and the Ginza District was the most popular destination for GIs on leave. The Ginza is an upscale area of Tokyo with a shopping promenade housing department stores, boutiques, restaurants, and coffee houses. Because of its location near the Imperial Palace, which was never bombed by the air force, it remained relatively intact at war's end. This was in stark contrast to the surrounding area, which had suffered catastrophic destruction. The subway ride from Irumagawa to Tokyo revealed that the fire bombings had leveled the area. Literally for mile after mile from my subway car, I saw no standing structures. The subway system and its rail tracks, however, survived the bombings relatively unscathed.

Life was good. The war was over, and I would soon be returning to the States in February or March of 1946 based on the number of "points" that I had accumulated. The point system was based on the number of months of military service, with extra points for months served overseas.

Then disaster struck!

I was on leave in Tokyo when I suddenly became very sick. I was overcome by weakness, felt faint, and had shaking chills. I was in such bad shape that my buddies knew I could not make it back to base, so they literally carried me to the Forty-Second General Hospital. Little did they or I know that the Forty-Second General Hospital was, in fact, known in peacetime as St. Luke's Medical Center. It was a world-renowned medical center. It had one thousand beds furnished with the latest medical equipment, and a medical staff with the most prestigious medical backgrounds. How lucky was I to have been carried to this facility?

It was quickly determined that I had come down with malaria.

By way of history, malaria reached epidemic proportions among American troops fighting the Japanese in the South Pacific, effectively neutralizing their combat abilities. Quinine had always been used to prevent and treat the disease. It is found in the root, bark, and branches of the cinchona tree. Unfortunately, our supply of these raw materials was cut off by the early Japanese conquests in the South Pacific.

Fortunately, however, in the 1930s, the first synthetic antimalarial drug had been developed and had been sold under the name of Atabrine. It was a bitter-tasting pill that turned your skin yellow and had some undesirable side effects. It was effective only if the GIs could be made to take it. So to ensure that the Atabrine was actually swallowed, soldiers stood at the head of mess lines to carefully watch each GI take his little yellow tablet.

I had taken my Atabrine religiously in New Guinea, Okinawa, and the Philippines, but after arrival in Japan, the medication was no longer required. But the Anopheles mosquito had fulfilled its deadly mission, and absent the therapeutic effects of the pill, I came down with malaria.

The one fortunate result was that the ongoing bouts of malaria classified me as a disabled veteran. As a disabled veteran (10 percent disabled), I qualified for significant student benefits over and above the generous benefits available to most GIs.

I spent fifteen days at the Forty-Second General Hospital and then returned to active duty and began writing letters to my congressman to speed my return to the States.

In late January 1946, I received my traveling orders. I shipped out of Yokohama, Japan, and after a stormy sea voyage, arrived in Seattle,

Washington, on February 9, 1946. A long train ride across the country carried me to my place of separation from the military, Fort Dix, New Jersey. Discharge from the armed forces took place on February 19, 1946, when I received my back pay and, best of all, a train ticket home to Buffalo, New York.

For me, World War II was over. Sixty-five years later, it is something I do not think about, but I will never forget.

LAW SCHOOL

1946–1949

I applied for admission to the University of Buffalo School of Law, and on April 16, 1946, thanks to all of the college credits I had accumulated at Hamilton College, I received notice that I had been accepted for the Class of 1949. Things were looking up! As a disabled veteran, not only was my tuition covered by the GI Bill, but also a book allowance, all student fees, and a small monthly disability pension was paid. I was living with Mom and Dad, and I was the proud owner of a 1936 Oldsmobile.

I was dating the love of my life, Mary, who was employed by the Donner Hanna Coke Corporation. She was only eighteen at the time, but thanks to her employment in the executive suites as a secretary, I had a well-paying summer job all of my law school years, maintaining the rail lines that serviced the coal cars. The employees of the plant had selected the United Steelworkers of America as their union, and union membership was required. My mandatory membership was to have wonderful and highly beneficial consequences a decade later.

Our law school freshman class totaled 122. The new law school was yet to be built, and initially our classes were located in an old

Victorian-style mansion, across the street from the Erie County Hall, which housed the county and state courts. In our junior and senior years, the school moved our classes to the Prudential Office Building, but our professors ignored our ignoble surroundings and taught us well the basics as well as the intricacies of the tort law, contract law, criminal law, domestic relations law, and so on.

I enjoyed my three years at the law school and had no trouble maintaining my grades. I was selected for law review in my senior year, which at the time I viewed as some kind of burden. Only later did I realize that it was, in fact, a very prestigious recognition of my classroom efforts.

Law school classes were not easy As. Only seventy-seven of the one hundred and twenty-two who had begun our studies in 1946 survived to graduate. Thirty-seven percent of that initial student body had flunked out.

The year 1949 was very memorable and eventful. Graduation from law school took place on June 1. I did not attend the actual graduation ceremony because I, and most of my classmates, were in New York City taking a bar review course. The New York State Bar examination is one of the nation's most difficult tests for admission to the practice of law, so the University of Buffalo Law School faculty highly recommended a bar review course of some type. I passed that hurdle and was admitted to the practice of law in the state of New York on November 3. But the most important and most significant event of the year was my marriage to the love of my life, Mary Dmitrzak, on August 20, 1949.

THE PRACTICE OF LAW

1949–1968

The one significant element law school does not teach is the practical application in the real world of all that education. Simple answers to questions like where does one enter a default judgment, file a deed, secure a search and survey for a real estate purchase or sale, and so forth are left for a later date.

After graduation I sought a clerkship in a law office that would allow me to master those everyday practical skills that I would need when I opened my own law office.

My uncle, Brunon Boroszewski, was an attorney in a solo practice and recommended me to the attorney he had clerked for, Eugene Blazejewski. It was a most propitious recommendation. Mr. Blazejewski was not only a very successful lawyer who soon taught me where the courthouse was and what to do when I got there, but as I soon discovered, he also was an active and very influential leader in the Democratic Party of western New York on the federal, state, county, and city levels.

Under Mr. Blazejewski's aegis, I was introduced to the everyday world behind the judicial facade. He made me aware of the important and mostly underestimated role that the support personnel in the civil, trial, and surrogate courts play in our court system. In their quiet, unassuming roles behind the scenes, they often control the court calendars, approve any documents requiring a judge's signature, and generally ensure that the court runs smoothly. A lawyer who is argumentative and does not treat them with the respect they think they deserve does so at his own peril. Those lawyers never do understand why, on those days when the judge has a long motion calendar, their cases were always the last to be heard. Mr. Blazejewski was very aware that when the court is in recess and the judge is in chambers relaxing with his staff, an offhand favorable or disparaging comment by a court reporter or a clerk about the ongoing case may many times unintentionally influence a decision in a case. Treating court people kindly and courteously is, in and of itself, one of the weapons a lawyer has at his disposal in becoming a winning trial lawyer. I learned early on, thanks to Mr. Blazejewski, that in addition to knowing the law and the practical basics of a law practice, treating court personnel courteously is a must for a successful practice.

My clerkship was not a well-paying position; fortunately, Mary had a well-paying secretarial position. Attorneys selected for clerkships with the larger law firms and with judges make attractive salaries, but in terms of life experiences, my clerkship opened up a treasure trove of connections and real-world knowledge that proved invaluable in my future.

Mr. Blazejewski, at every opportunity, gave me opportunities to stretch my legal wings. Law clerkships have many similarities with medical residencies and internships. Both fields provide wonderful learning experiences but at a price—long hours with little financial remuneration.

Mr. Blazejewski's office was the gathering place for our congressman, T. J. Dulski, who represented the Forty-First District in the state of New York; the incumbent mayor; county and city officials; and a fair number of federal officials serving in the Truman administration. On an informal basis, they were planning the next campaign—discussing future campaign issues, and of course, the necessary financing. As a very, very young attorney, I felt privileged to be a part of their discussions, but more important, the office was a very important school in teaching me Politics 101, Politics 102, Politics 103, and Politics 104.

Besides helping me learn the business of law, Mr. Blazejewski played a very active role in any campaign that was going on, and of course I tagged along, learning how our great democracy works at the retail and grassroots levels.

I was all-too-eager to make a run for political office. My prayers were soon answered A neighbor, John McGuire, was very upset with policies being formulated by the Board of Education of the Maryvale School District, where we resided. Policy making is the responsibility of the Board of Education, which is duly elected by the people of the district. John was sure that as a team, we could unseat the incumbents, and I saw no need to disagree with him.

We won handily, and I was sworn in as a member of the Maryvale School District Board of Education. The school district was in desperate need of a new high school, which the board authorized, funded, and constructed. In honor of my board position overseeing the construction of the high school, a large brass plaque in the school lobby now bears my name and the names of the other board members.

My next successful campaign was for committeeman representing my neighbors on Smallwood Terrace in the town of Cheektowaga, where Mary and I had bought a home. The town charter required two committee persons, so I teamed up with one of our good neighbors, Ms. Edna Mae Klinshaw. Our opposition was two elderly gentlemen who had held these posts for years, and they were not ready to give up their positions to a couple of young whippersnappers. It was a surprisingly tough and rigorous campaign for a position that paid no money and had little influence on the community. But Edna and I succeeded and took our positions as bona fide members of the Cheektowaga Democratic Town Committee.

To be a campaign manager was a big step forward, so when a friend and aspiring politician asked me to manage his campaign against our incumbent supervisor, I readily accepted. It was to be my next tour de force. My earlier victories coupled with my youthful inexperience had given my ego a big boost and as a result, hope and enthusiasm overruled good judgment. The incumbent and his well-oiled political organization trounced us badly.

In defeat, I learned many lessons about the values inherent in a well-disciplined political party machine. Mary took the defeat very well, I suspect almost gleefully, although she would never admit it. Happiness, for her, was no more noisy political meetings in her basement. Mary was not a political person, but she patiently put up with all of my political ventures.

SOLO PRACTICE

I was admitted to the bar on November 3, 1949, and I was ready to open up my own law office. Mr. Blazejewski warned me that the first year would be difficult financially, but if I could survive the first year of solo practice, the practice would support me. He also made it very clear that if I needed any help, his door was always open.

In the early 1950s, a significant number of attorneys in the Buffalo area maintained law offices in the neighborhood where they lived, rather than in a formal office building. Some opted for a storefront location, but most remodeled the front porch of their homes to accommodate their law practice.

An office building location was beyond my rental budget, and I did not own a home on a busy thoroughfare, so the only viable option was a storefront. I found a suitable storefront on one of Buffalo's main streets, Broadway. It was next to a busy barber shop, so I felt assured that there would be ample foot traffic. So in early 1950 I made a small investment in desks, chairs, telephones, and a typewriter, and I was in business.

My instincts were correct, and within a matter of weeks, thanks to the lessons learned during my clerkship with Mr. Blazejewski, I was drawing wills, closing real estate contracts, preparing tax returns, collecting debts, and performing other small, but profitable, legal activities that were not a part of but were an application of my law school studies.

My law business income continued to improve slowly but surely, and for the first time, I believed I could support my family without having to rely on my wife's salary. This was excellent timing, because Mary was pregnant, and our blessed event would take place in December. Deborah was born on December 14. It was to be a beautiful and glorious end for the year 1950, which it was, except for the sadness following the death of my father on Christmas day.

Suddenly, and out of nowhere, fate again intervened to dramatically change the nature and scope of my law practice.

THE UNITED STEELWORKERS
OF AMERICA

Describing this event requires a flashback to the year 1942. My uncle, Dr. John Boroszewski, had rented a cottage at Idlewood Shores on Lake Erie. His wife, Helen, was having some health problems, so he asked my mother, his sister, if she would be willing to be his wife's caregiver that summer. It was understood that she would be accompanied by her four children. My mother agreed and I, my two brothers, and my sister were off to Idlewood for the summer.

An attorney, J. Harry Tiernan and his wife, Lucia, rented a cottage across the street. Over the summer, the children of the two families became great friends, spending our vacations at the beach or on the tennis courts.

Flash forward ten years to the fall of 1952. I am sitting in my storefront office, the telephone rings, I answer, and a voice identifies the caller as Harry Tiernan—a voice from the past.

Fifty-seven years later, I can still recall the elation I felt when he asked me if I would be interested in associating myself with him in providing workers' compensation legal assistance for every major steelworker union in the metropolitan Buffalo area.

Wow!

I had not seen Mr. Tiernan in the last ten years. I had no experience in workers' compensation law. I had no idea why he had selected me. Nevertheless, I said *yes*.

To work out the details Mr. Tiernan suggested that we meet at my home that evening at 7:00 p.m.. Any time or date would have been acceptable to me! In any event, I closed the office early to tell Mary of our good fortune and prepared for the meeting. I was anxious to make a good impression, and since I was driving a beat-up Chevrolet, I decided to park it around the corner. When Mr. Tiernan drove up a few minutes before seven, I knew I had guessed correctly. He drove up in a Lincoln Continental. I was impressed.

The meeting went surprisingly well. Whatever terms or conditions he would propose for our partnership, I was prepared to accept. He was extremely generous in proposing that all fees received and expenses incurred be divided equally. I could not believe my good fortune! I had about one year of actual law practice, which was going well, but nothing to compare with what the future could hold. The Buffalo metropolitan area in the early 1950s was a vibrant industrial complex, dominated by the steel and auto industries. They were highly unionized, and my future partner had signed agreements to represent all of the employees of such industrial giants like Bethlehem Steel, Republic Steel, and the Donner Hanna Corporation, where Mary had been employed and where I had once had a summer job. The list of corporations was lengthy, but the few I mention illustrate the numbers involved.

Mr. Tiernan said he was in need of a partner because his existing partner was retiring. I could not help but ask why he had selected me. I was about the same age as his children, and he was about my father's age. He related that he had remembered me from the Idlewood days and had observed my handling of a case of which I had no recollection. He thought it made good sense for him to associate himself with a younger lawyer that he could train in his procedures and that as he grew older would allow him to work at an easier pace. It turns out that I was the only young lawyer he knew and had some confidence in.

As soon as he left, Mary and I danced and laughed with great abandon. Suddenly the door bell rang. It was Mr. Tiernan. His Lincoln Continental would not start. He needed a ride to the nearest garage. Well, so much for the best-laid plans. I went around the corner, started my car, and drove him to the garage. He was so concerned about getting his Lincoln going that I am sure he paid no attention to the age or condition of my Chevrolet.

I closed my office, moved my furniture to my basement, and moved to my new offices in the Edwards Building. As I entered my new offices, it was difficult for me to grasp that I now officially represented all of the fifty thousand men and women who were members of the United Steelworkers of America, Region IV.

WORKERS' COMPENSATION LAW

Workers' compensation is a form of insurance that provides compensation and medical care for employees who are injured in the course of employment. Payments, usually biweekly, are intended to replace wages lost. In addition, injuries that result in permanent physical limitations may be reimbursed by a lump sum payment in lieu of the weekly payments. In return, the employee relinquishes his or her right to sue the employer.

The transition from my solo practice to a workers' compensation practice with J. Harry was smooth, quick, and easy, not only because J. Harry was a good teacher, but primarily because his good humor, legal skills, and outgoing personality made each day's work a real pleasure and something I looked forward to. In the decade following, I established a reputation as having some expertise in workers' compensation, and our practice prospered.

I, however, had not lost my political aspirations, and my association with the Steelworkers Union opened up new doors at a much higher political level.

The director of the United Steelworkers Union, Region IV, was Joseph P. Molony, and he had jurisdiction over all steelworker unions in the state of New York. In the 1960s he was elected international vice president of the United Steelworkers of America. Where Mr. Blazejewski's political contacts were at the retail, or local level, Mr. Molony's contacts were at the wholesale, or the state and national levels.

Mr. Molony's offices were adjacent to mine, and in the ordinary course of my workers' compensation practice, including staff meetings and Christmas parties, I worked with and came to know him and all of the local union presidents. Most of the union presidents were old enough to be my father, and I was a twenty-something-year-old lawyer young enough to be their son. As a result of this providentially symbiotic relationship, coupled with the favorable comments from their injured union members that I had represented, these union presidents began requesting that I represent their local unions in arbitration hearings, contract negotiations, and other labor relations matters. The additional income was most welcome.

My involvement in these statewide labor issues allowed me to be present at all Region IV staff meetings scheduled by Mr. Molony throughout the state of New York. When meetings were scheduled in New York City or at the state capital, Mr. Molony, who became my mentor in the field of labor law, made sure that I accompanied him, including when, in the course of union business, he met with such historic figures as Nelson Rockefeller, Averill Harriman, New York City Mayor Wagner, and my old friend Congressman Thaddeus Dulski.

John F. Kennedy was elected president of the United States in November of 1960. In the western New York area, normally Republican cities such as Niagara Falls and Rochester had voted overwhelmingly Democratic. The time seemed ripe for me to run for judicial office. The Erie County judgeship in 1962 would have no incumbent, and even though Erie County was considered a safe Republican seat, I felt that the impetus of the Kennedy election made the election of a Democratic candidate feasible.

I unashamedly used all my political connections to get the nomination, and in the spring of 1962, the Erie County Democratic Committee unanimously endorsed me as their nominee for the position of Erie County judge. I was jubilant. A strong and passionate Democratic wave was sweeping the country and Erie County in particular, and the political pundits considered my election a foregone conclusion.

Then disaster struck the Democratic Party in Buffalo, New York. In the primary election of 1962, the incumbent mayor of Buffalo, Frank Sedita, was defeated in a bitter primary campaign by my fellow classmate and political unknown Victor Manz. Mayor Sedita would "not go gently into that good night" but decided to run in the general election as an independent on the "Liberty Bell" label. As the incumbent mayor and putative leader of a large Democratic metropolitan area, he was able to marshal all those invisible inchoate forces present in the phrase "you can't fight city hall" in support of his candidacy. The large Democratic voting majorities usually associated with the city of Buffalo were split between the Democratic ticket and the Liberty Bell Sedita ticket.

The entire Democratic ticket in Buffalo went down to a resounding defeat, while Democratic tickets in Niagara Falls, Rochester, and so forth were elected by the overwhelming majorities I had anticipated for Buffalo. I often wonder how different my life would have been if not for the totally unexpected intervention of fate by way of a mayor's primary race.

The 1950s were a wonderful decade in my life. First and most important, Mary and I were blessed with the birth of four wonderful children. On December 14, 1950, my daughter Deborah was born.

She is now a vice president with the *Chicago Tribune* newspaper chain. Frank was born on September 5, 1953. His forte is computers, and he is technical services manager for the Spectral Response Corporation. Claudia was born on July 8, 1956. She completed her medical school studies and is now a board-certified anesthesiologist. Jim was born on July 6, 1958. He is now a professor of biochemistry at New York University.

The 1960s were to be a decade of change both geographically and career-wise. The national economy was experiencing significant changes that slowly but surely transformed the western New York economy into what many writers have dubbed the "Rust Belt." Looking back, it is hard to believe that industry giants that employed our retainer base, such as Bethlehem Steel, Republic Steel, Symington Gould Foundry, and so on, were forced to close their doors. It was not a quick and dramatic change in Buffalo's industrial picture, but rather a slow and painful plant-by-plant loss of jobs and production. The sorrowful plight of my unemployed clients made me appreciate that their financial predicament was, to a considerable degree, mitigated by such measures as our union pension agreements, unemployment insurance, and Social Security. This heady dose of reality was to have a profound influence on my future.

In the fall of 1967, one of the local union presidents asked if I would represent one of his disabled members at a hearing for Social Security disability benefits. This type of representation was not covered by our retainer agreement, but I believed that it would certainly build goodwill with the union president and his members, so I agreed to accept the case. This spur-of-the-moment, relatively unimportant decision was to have momentous consequences.

The Social Security hearing was scheduled on what turned out to be a raw, cold, and snowy November day. I had no prior experience with

Social Security hearings, but I believed that my wealth of experience in workers' compensation disability cases would serve me in good stead. My assumption was correct, and the hearing went very smoothly to its favorable conclusion.

The hearing was held before Herbert Ferguson, a hearing examiner (now administrative law judge) with the Bureau of Hearing and Appeals of the Social Security Administration. It was Ferguson's last hearing of the day, it was bitterly cold outside, and being in no hurry, I remarked that he must be anxious to return to his home office in Atlanta, Georgia. He, of course, answered in the affirmative and briefly described his work with the Social Security Administration and his offices on Peachtree Street in Atlanta. The words "Peachtree Street" hit a nerve. On this frigid Buffalo day, I envisioned an avenue flanked with leafy fruit trees ripe with juicy peaches ready to be picked by any pedestrian.

He volunteered that his hearing examiner position was the only position in government filled by attorneys who have qualified for appointment by successfully passing a three-part examination based upon the following—a proven seven-year history of trial experience, a test involving the writing of a decision, and a panel interview conducted under the aegis of the US Civil Service Commission. Those selected were given a lifetime appointment, subject to removal only for cause. The salary paid was remarkably competitive with my current income.

In light of the current decline in Buffalo's industrial economy, I immediately thought it might be in my best interests to qualify for this position. The names of the attorneys who successfully passed the examination were placed on a register maintained by the US Civil Service Commission, and as individual agencies required the employment of hearing examiners, the register was forwarded to the employing agency. An attorney could decline the offer of employment by an agency with no penalty. His or her name would remain on the register. To have a backup position such as this in the event of some future unforeseeable events was to me to have the best of all worlds.

Herbert Ferguson supplied me with an address where the appropriate applications could be secured, and as I left the courthouse, the weather outside did not seem as cold, and I could almost smell the peaches.

Hearing examiners, I soon discovered, were used by various government agencies, such as the National Labor Relations Board, the Interstate Commerce Commission, the Department of Agriculture, the Federal Trade Commission, the Social Security Administration, and so forth, but regardless of the agency they were employed by, each hearing examiner had to be screened and certified for appointment by the Office of Personnel Management. To qualify for the position of hearing examiner, each applicant must at the time of filing have been duly licensed to practice law and at least seven years of actual trial experience If an applicant met this initial hurdle, the applicant then had to score eighty out of one hundred total points based on the following tests: the writing of a written decision, favorable peer recommendations from the attorneys who had opposed the applicant in the cases submitted to establish seven years of trial experience, and an evaluation by a three-member panel composed of a an OPM representative, an agency executive, and an individual from a private law firm.

Hearing examiners are the only judges in the US government who are selected solely on the basis of merit.

Once appointed, hearing examiners are totally insulated from bureaucratic pressures from the agency, where they serve to guarantee their total impartiality as decision makers.

Illustrative of this is the following statement published by the Center for Administrative Justice:[3] "It is our view that public trust in the SSA scheme of social insurance would be significantly undermined were the opportunity for a face-to-face encounter with a demonstrably independent decision maker was eliminated from the system."

The Congress, to ensure the independence of the judicial proceedings and to guarantee constitutional due process, enacted the Administrative Procedure Act[4] (APA). This legislation governs the practice and proceedings before all federal administrative agencies to minimize bureaucratic arbitrariness and overreaching.

The APA provides that upon appointment, new hearing examiners are not subject to any probationary period before permanent appointment; they are exempt from performance evaluations; and upon appointment, hearing examiners becomes permanent members of the agency and can only be removed for "good cause." OPM establishes the hearing examiner's salary, independent of any ranking or appraisal by the agency. A hearing examiner cannot be assigned any duties that would be inconsistent with the position of hearing examiner. In addition, hearing examiners are to be assigned cases on a rotating basis.

To avoid any suspicion or the appearance of collusion between the hearing examiner and agency personnel, the hearing examiner may *not* be responsible to, or subject to, the supervision of anyone in the agency performing investigative or prosecutorial functions.

---

3   *Study of the Social Security Administration Hearing System*, October 1977, pp. xxii, xxiii. (Center for Administrative Justice, later published by Heath and Company, Lexington, Massachusetts, 1978).

4   Administrative Procedure Act (5 U.S.C.A. §§ 551-706).

In exchange for this extraordinary freedom and independence, hearing examiners are expected to perform their adjudicatory duties in a manner consistent with the letter and spirit of the Administrative Procedure Act.

But I digress. I filed all the requisite papers with my application, and they passed muster. The next step was to write a proper judicial decision. In a relatively short period of time, I was notified to appear at the main post office in Buffalo, New York, for that purpose.

I made sure that I arrived on time as directed and was quickly escorted into one of the post office's examination rooms. The monitor gave me short and simple instructions. I was to be supplied with a college-type blue book in which to write a decision. An insert in the blue book described the facts of a case that I discovered later had been taken from an actual case decided in one of the circuit courts of appeals. It had not been a unanimous decision, so there was no right or wrong answer. I was to be allowed five hours to write my decision, based upon the record supplied, beginning now!

It took about an hour to digest and study the factual record and then decide what the applicable law was and how it should be applied to the given state of facts. The hours flew by, and with about ten minutes remaining, I delivered my decision and all papers to the exam monitor.

My decision evidently met OPM's high standards, and shortly thereafter I appeared before the three-member evaluation panel.

They must have reported favorably, because as my family and I were preparing to celebrate our Easter vacation in Florida, I received a letter offering me employment and lifetime tenure as a hearing examiner with the Bureau of Hearing and Appeals Office in Atlanta, Georgia.

I had, of course, discussed the possibility of my being offered federal employment with my good friend, mentor, and partner, J. Harry Tiernan. We had worked together for twenty years, and in those two decades it is hard to believe we never had a disagreement or a cross word. We discussed our declining retainer base and the future of our practice, and sadly agreed that if offered federal employment, I should accept.

Mary, emotionally, was not sure about leaving Buffalo and moving to Atlanta. In our annual trips to Florida, she was terrified by Atlanta traffic. Once we were within the city limits of Atlanta, she would close her eyes and not reopen them until Atlanta was in our rearview mirror.

Pragmatically, when Mary considered the necessity of our family having a secure and adequate income for the foreseeable future and the looming prospects of providing a college education for our four children, her good judgment prevailed, and she reluctantly endorsed our family's move to Atlanta.

I forwarded my registered letter, return receipt requested, accepting the Social Security Administration's offer of employment.

NEW BEGINNING

~

On May 6, 1968, the director of the Bureau of Hearings and Appeals administered the following oath of office to me and the forty-two other members of the hearing examiner class of 1968:

> *I will support and defend the Constitution of the*
> *United States against all enemies, foreign and*
> *domestic; that I will bear true faith and allegiance*
> *to the same; that I take this obligation freely, without*
> *any mental reservation or purpose of evasion; and that*
> *I will well and faithfully discharge the duties of the office*
> *on which I am about to enter. So help me God.*

Events happened very quickly after my swearing in. Fortunately, all of the children were able to complete their classes without any mid-year interruption. The sale of our home went very smoothly, and we were able to close the sale one week before our departure for Atlanta.

The classes began on May 6, 1968. No one in the class had any experience or practical knowledge of the complexities of the Social Security law and its regulations, but when we graduated on June 28, we all had acquired an expertise that would serve us well in the years to come.

Equally important was a working understanding of the usual causes of disability, which required knowledge of orthopedics, neurology, psychiatry, and so forth, and understanding how to apply this knowledge in deciding Social Security disability cases. Amazingly, after eight weeks of medical lectures by specialists in their respective fields, we certainly were not MDs, but we had enough background knowledge to deal comfortably with those medical issues when they came up in the course of a trial.

The week after graduation was hectic, as we had to be in Atlanta on July 6. The house was sold. Mary had done yeoman's work in closing out our utility accounts, hand packing most of the breakables, and arranging a moving date. The movers arrived on schedule on July 2 and packed our worldly goods, and by 4:00 p.m. the van was on its way to put our goods into a storage facility in Atlanta. Our home was empty, so that night we camped in, sleeping on the floor. Luckily it was carpeted. On July 3 we were on our way to Atlanta.

ATLANTA, GEORGIA

～

We found a motel a block from my offices at Peachtree Road and Fifth Street. Until we purchased a new home, I was able to walk to work, which freed up our automobile for Mary. Happily, as long as she did not have to drive on the interstates, she was able to cope with Atlanta traffic. On August 20, we moved into our new home at 3940 Granger Drive. This move facilitated the enrollment of our children into some excellent neighborhood schools.

Upon entering my new offices, I was greeted by none other than Herbert Ferguson, who was truly responsible for the chain of events that had led me to Atlanta. He had lived most of his life in Atlanta and made it his personal responsibility to make sure that my family would be comfortable there. He was a great help in our search for a home and in explaining the office routines. His home was only a few blocks away from mine, so we were able to carpool to work. Mary was most happy to have an automobile at her disposal when I drove in with Ferguson.

HEARING EXAMINER

A few months after my entry on duty, I was handling a full docket of cases. The Social Security laws and regulations relative to disability were not too dissimilar from the New York State Workmen's Compensation statutes, and as a result, my transition from being an advocate in a disability case to deciding a disability case was easy.

By way of background, Congress enacted the Social Security Act in 1935.[5] It created a trust fund financed by employee and employer contributions to provide benefits for retired workers at age sixty-five. In subsequent years, Congress passed legislation that provided Social Security benefits to younger workers who had worked at least ten years and who were permanently and totally disabled.

To gain passage of the Social Security Act, a trade-off took place in Congress where amazingly, the individual states and *not* the Social Security Administration made the initial disability determinations. The state operations would be fully funded by the Social Security Administration, but strangely their disability decisions would *not* be based on the Social Security law and regulations but on a "manual" that attempts to interpret the Social Security law and regulations.

---

5   Social Security Act, Chapter 531, 49 Stat. 620 (1935).

This strange anomaly in the law persists to this day and continues to cause significant operational problems for the Social Security Administration, since the manual has no legal standing or validity, and the administrative law judges and the courts cannot use or reference it in their decisions.

In 1972 Congress enacted legislation creating the Supplemental Security Insurance Program,[6] which extended benefits to individuals who were disabled but had no relevant work history and who had not contributed to the trust fund. These payments would be made from general tax revenues but would be administered by the Social Security Administration.

In all of these programs, no benefits were paid for a partial disability. To qualify for benefits, one had to prove that he or she was totally and permanently disabled. The Social Security regulations[7] in substance defined a disabled person as one who is not only unable to do his or her previous work, *but cannot do any other type of work,* regardless of whether such other work even exists in the area where he or she lives or whether an actual job vacancy exists. To illustrate, a teacher who had severe orthopedic problems who could not stand the required number of hours to teach a class but medically was able to sit on a stool at a movie theater to sell and dispense tickets would not qualify for disability benefits even if there were no theaters in the town.

Thus, there are two ultimate issues that must be addressed in every Social Security disability case, which constitute the majority of cases heard by the Bureau of Hearings and Appeals. First, what medical impairments are present, and second, do they prevent the claimant from engaging in any type of work?

---

6   Social Security Amendments of 1973, Public Law No. 92-603.

7   42 U.S.C. § 416(i)(i).

I had hardly settled in to my new offices when I was visited by my regional chief hearing examiner, Larry Goodman. He was not pleased with the administrative operation of the Atlanta Hearing Office and desired to make some changes in policy and personnel. He had reviewed my résumé and believed that my history in directing the legal activities of a major industrial union was the type of leadership he required to turn his largest hearing office into a more effective unit. Modestly, I protested that I had just arrived, and I was still learning the nuances of the Social Security disability program. In turn, Larry replied that my Social Security skills would improve with time, but what he needed now was a person with proven administrative skills to run the office.

On May 10, 1969, twelve months after my appointment as a hearing examiner, I found myself in charge of the largest hearing office in the southeastern United States.

I must admit that I had always enjoyed the administrative challenges in running any organization, and with these tweaks, the Atlanta office was operating smoothly. More important, Larry seemed to be pleased with our monthly reports on morale and productivity.

Basically, a number of operational problems that hampered the decisional processes of the individual hearing examiners in the Atlanta Hearing Office had to be addressed.

For background, to fully understand the nature of these problems, it should be understood that the hearing examiner usually had no difficulty in establishing what medical disabilities the claimant was alleging in support of his claim for disability benefits.

The more difficult and complex question in establishing the presence of a disability was whether these impairments were severe enough to prevent the claimant from engaging in any type of work.

Deciding the presence of a disability under the Social Security law is the most elusive and complicated determination ever devised by man in any judicial or quasi-judicial legal system.

In reaching a decision in an individual case, the hearing examiner must consider elements of medicine, subjective complaints of pain, the existence of work, and the uniqueness of the individual claimant. A finding of disability is thus a legal conclusion, not a medical decision or a sociological theory or a philosophical premise. By definition, a disability claim does not lend itself to mass adjudication, as each decision must be tailored to the individual claimant.

One learned writer[8] had difficulty coming to terms with the Social Security definition of disability when he stated, "Much of the difficulty of defining disability results from a confused and even contradictory philosophical base used to justify the program in our economically competitive society."

Further complicating the work of a hearing examiner in deciding a case is the level of proof a claimant must submit to prevail. The Social Security statute and applicable regulations state that there must be *substantial* evidence to support a favorable finding of disability. What is substantial evidence?

---

8   See Lance Liebman, "The definition of disability in Social Security and Supplemental Security Income: Drawing the Bounds of Social Welfare Estates," *Harvard Law Review*, 89 (March 1976): 883.

The US Supreme Court, in the case of *Consolidated Edison Co. v. NLRB (305 US 197)*, defined *substantial* evidence as more than a mere scintilla. It means such relevant evidence as a reasonable mind might accept as adequate to support a conclusion and that rational individuals will normally rely upon such evidence in conducting their daily affairs. *(See Richardson v. Perales 405 US 389.)*

Substantial evidence is less than a *preponderance* of the evidence and certainly far less than *beyond a reasonable doubt*. If preponderance is assumed to be more than 51 percent, what percentage should be assigned to substantial evidence?

To assist the hearing examiner in sorting out all of the medical and employment issues, the Bureau of Hearings and Appeals has retained a cadre of "vocational experts" to give testimony at the individual hearings.

The hearing begins with the claimant giving testimony as to his age, education, and work history and how his medical problems prevent him from returning to any kind of work. In complex medical situations, the hearing examiner may request that a medical expert testify about whether the record supports the existence of any medically determinable impairment. With this background data in hand, the hearing examiner propounds a hypothetical question for the vocational expert. This hypothetical question will include all relevant data, such as the claimant's age, education, work history, and most important, a summary of the claimant's impairments and the degree of physical and psychological limitations they impose upon him or her. The question concludes by asking the vocational expert to assume the validity of all of the findings and conclusions in the hypothetical statement and requests that the expert "identify any jobs or work, if any, that an individual as identified in the hypothetical question could perform."

The problem in the Atlanta hearing office was that the vocational expert would give a knowledgeable reply, but in many instances the rationale or basis for his expert opinion was not well articulated for easy inclusion in the hearing examiner's decision. To remedy the situation, I scheduled a joint conference with the hearing examiners and the entire vocational expert cadre. With the able assistance and valuable input from Professor Richard M. Smith and Professor John D. Blakeman, we prepared an agenda for the meeting. As a result, once the vocational experts were aware of the hearing examiners' frustration with their rationales, they formulated the following solution, which was enthusiastically adopted by all parties.

The group decided that, first and most important, all significant words, such as *work*, *job*, and *job description*, should be defined so that all parties were singing from the same songbook. This was formulated by the group with the following definitions:

Work is the sustained performance for wages,
1. of specific physical and/or intellectual functions,
2. during a fixed period of time,
3. to meet a competitive standard of performance, under supervision,
4. at a place designated by an employer, and
5. in a setting characterized by certain interpersonal, intrapersonal, and environmental conditions.

Job is a specific type of kind or work.

Job description is unique to a single employer, industry, or place of business.

VE opinion must be based on four factors—age, education, past work, and impairments as given or formulated by the Hearing Examiner and should incorporate the following:

1. Definition of work as per the above definition.
2. Expert opinion—i.e., past relevant jobs, other jobs, or no jobs.
3. Rationale:
   a. This should touch on each of the factors contained in the definitions that are relevant or have application to the issues. Be specific.
   b. This should include such other relevant data as may be pertinent to the issues.
4. Discussion of what major vocational adjustments if any would be required because of age or other factors.

All the parties agreed that the above framework would provide the hearing examiner with the necessary rationale for inclusion in a decision and also provide the VEs with a workable formula when giving testimony at a hearing.

The other problem involved the skill level and physical requirements of thirty-seven jobs indigenous to the state of Georgia. Vocational experts from the University of Georgia in Athens differed in the classification of many of these jobs with the vocational experts from Georgia State University in Atlanta. As a result, the geographic location of the VE selected to testify at the hearing could determine the decision.

Once the VEs were made aware of the problem, they quickly reviewed the job titles and submitted an amended list, which established uniform skill levels and physical requirements.

In one meeting, problems solved.

THE ASSOCIATION OF
HEARING EXAMINERS IN DHEW

L ong before my arrival on the scene, the three-hundred-plus hearing examiners employed by the Social Security Administration had formed an organization, the Association of Hearing Examiners in the Department of Health, Education, and Welfare to deal with the bureaucracy from which they were insulated by the Administrative Procedures Act of 1947.[9]

The past leadership had two principal concerns. First was the matter of pay. By some accident of history, the hearing examiners in the Social Security Administration had been ranked as GS-15s, while all other hearing examiners in federal employment were ranked one grade higher, as GS-16s. Second was the matter of job description. Dissatisfaction with the job title was a source of irritation to hearing examiners in all agencies. They uniformly believed that the job title did not adequately describe their duties and that a more accurate title would be administrative law judge.

The problem, of course, was that their employing agencies had nothing to do with either problem. The only agency that could change

---

9   Administrative Procedure Act (5 U.S.C.A. §§ 551-706).

their pay and title status was the Civil Service Commission (now the Office of Personnel Management).

I could not have foreseen that the many friends I had made in my union and political lives would so quickly affect my future. The corps of hearing examiners had been totally frustrated in their attempts to correct what they believed were their pay and title problems. Herb Ferguson, who had an active role in the association, figured out from our conversation during our daily commutes that I had been active politically and that one of my good congressional friends in the Buffalo area was T. J. Dulski. I did not know that my friend T. J. Dulski was the chairman of the Post Office and Civil Service Committees. Herb Ferguson did.

In the spring of 1971, the Association of Hearing Examiners in the Department of Health, Education, and Welfare was scheduled to elect its president for the year. Herbert Ferguson made it his business to persuade his colleagues in the association to nominate me for the office. It was his considered judgment and advice to his fellow hearing examiners that it might be in their best interests to elect as their president a hearing examiner who, although young, inexperienced, and new to the Social Security system, had access to the chairman of the one congressional committee that could introduce legislation dealing with pay and title.

I was elected.

I served two terms as president of the association, and the Board of Governors and I routinely met with director of the Bureau of Hearings and Appeals. Again, my good fortune of being associated with such outstanding individuals as Blazejewski, Tiernan, Molony, and Ferguson continued. Shortly before my election as president, H. Dale Cook was appointed director of the Bureau of Hearings and Appeals.

Dale Cook and I were both veterans, we shared the same birth year, and where I had served as counsel for the steelworkers, his legal career encompassed private practice, employment as the first assistant US attorney in Oklahoma City, and work as legal counsel and advisor to then Oklahoma Governor Henry Bellmon. Most important, he was a legal scholar who was truly dedicated to the rule of law. The Fourth of July was his favorite holiday, and each year he read the Declaration of Independence to his family. We hit it off immediately.

My history in labor relations began to pay immediate dividends. I had always recognized that there was a natural tension between employees and management. Management, by definition, was responsible to its shareholders—and in government to the taxpayers—to be effective and productive. To me, productivity was not a term of opprobrium. Productivity was one of the hallmarks of efficiency and evidence of a well-run operation by management. Without profits, jobs would not exist for the people I represented. Historically, I had viewed my primary duty in negotiating union contracts with management as ending up with a labor agreement that provided employees not only with a competitive wage but a safe and stable environment that would promote morale and productivity. These goals were not incompatible with maintaining the production and direction requirements of management. Any labor-management agreement that would encourage and abet "feather bedding" or other similar practices would in the long run spell disaster for both the employer and the employees I represented.

This philosophy had served me well for two decades representing the steelworkers, and I felt confident that it would serve me equally well as the president of the Association of Hearing Examiners in the Department of Health, Education, and Welfare.

As vindication of that philosophy, not only was the Atlanta Office of Hearings and Appeals the regional leader in productivity, but not inconsequentially, morale and esprit de corps were high.

On one occasion, I was asked to lead a management team in negotiating a labor agreement with the clerical employees employed by the Bureau of Hearings and Appeals in Region IV of the Social Security Administration. It was a strange role for an attorney who had previously only represented unions. The employees were represented by Ms. Mary Smith, who was employed as a hearing assistant in the Lexington, Kentucky, office and who had led the effort for union representation. She was to become the first president of the American Federation of Government Employees (AFGE) Local Union 3627. She had been assisted in her unionization efforts by Ms. Elizabeth Scott, who was destined to be the executive vice president of the local union. The negotiations were scheduled to begin in Cincinnati, Ohio, on a Wednesday morning. Ms. Smith was represented and assisted by Thomas C. Bullington, the national representative for the AFGE.

Because of my long involvement in labor relations matters, I was fully familiar with the rituals and posturing involved in such negotiations, especially during the first days of the process, when the routine items, the so-called boilerplate, were negotiated. All went very smoothly until the matter of an arbitration clause submitted by the union came up for discussion. Both parties had different views as to its meaning and substance and went through the usual Kabuki dances defending or excoriating its provisions. It appeared that our management team and the union's national representative and his team were headed for an impasse in our contract deliberations. An impasse would probably translate into additional negotiations that could take an entire year, and in a worst-case scenario for the union, or maybe best-case scenario for management, no signed agreement ever. All this interminable delay over an arbitration clause that could not come into play for at least two years. I voiced these concerns to all parties as we adjourned our Thursday negotiations.

That evening, Ms. Smith met with her executive board, and over the objections of her national representative, decided that the importance of leaving Cincinnati with a signed contract was more important than, as I had suggested, extended meetings over a matter that had no immediate relevance.

Friday morning, she advised my management team of the executive's board decision, and Ms. Smith signed the proposed contract on behalf of her union. Mr. Bullington, visibly upset, refused to sign, but this did not affect the validity of the basic agreement. Ironically, I got the distinct impression that the management types at my own headquarters were not all that pleased with my expeditious handling of these negotiations. They seemed to be more interested in Kabuki dancing than the resolution of a labor/management agreement.

That afternoon, however, I was at the Cincinnati airport headed for home with a signed contract in my pocket. Years later, Ms. Smith encountered me at a meeting to thank me for my good and honest counsel that Thursday afternoon. Events had proceeded exactly as I had predicted. The disputed arbitration clause never came into play the first years of her presidency, and when a new contract was eventually negotiated, an acceptable arbitration clause was routinely accepted by all parties.

A NEW TITLE

The Social Security Administration's Bureau of Hearings and Appeals had by far the largest number of hearing examiners. The National Labor Relations Board (NLRB) had far fewer but still considerably more than any of the other federal agencies. The NLRB had always been in the forefront in dealing with the Civil Service Commission and the congressional committees to advance the independence and status of the hearing examiner corps. Being located in the Washington DC area, they were well positioned geographically and technically to represent the hearing examiner corps.

The hearing examiners in the DC area had formed their own association, the Federal Trial Examiners Conference. George L. Powell, a hearing examiner with the NLRB, was its president, and Gordon J. Myatt and John D. Gregg were the co-chairmen of its Legislative Committee.

In 1970, the conference had, under the leadership of George Powell, presented a number of title change position papers to the Civil Service Commission advocating that the commission approve and sponsor legislation changing the title from hearing examiner to administrative trial judge.

In 1953, the US Supreme Court in *Ramspeck v. Federal Trial Examiners' Conference*, 345 US 128, noted that hearing examiners have a special status that must be protected against incursions by agency executives, but the agencies successfully opposed and rejected any change in title to administrative law judge as recommended by the Hoover Task Force in 1955 because of the following:

- The decisional independence inherent in the title of judge would have a constraining and limiting influence on the scope of agency initiatives and policies.
- The change would lead to possible confusion with Article III judges.
- The respect and dignity that the judge title would command when reversing an agency determination would undermine the authority of the agency.
- The job title would adversely affect the ability of the agency to monitor the productivity of its judges.

Gordon Myatt and I had occasion to meet in Washington DC, and we quickly recognized that our two major organizations representing the vast majority of hearing examiners in federal employment had to join forces to secure a change in job title from the Civil Service Commission. Working together we believed that a new job title, which had for so long eluded us, was attainable.

The Washington DC hearing examiners had done all of the important and invaluable preparatory work in terms of position papers to justify a title change. Gordon and I agreed that the Association of Hearing Examiners in the Department of Health, Education, and Welfare, having hearing examiners located in all of the states except Alaska, would immediately meet with members' congressional contacts and request that the Civil Service Commission approve a change in title, while the hearing examiners in the Washington DC area would continue to file additional position and technical documents and use their proximity to the Civil Service Commission to advance our mutual cause for a change in title.

Such a two-pronged approach, we believed, would be successful. It was a marriage made in heaven!

On January 15, 1971, Congressman Dulski arranged for me, Association President Ben D. Worcester, George Powell, Gordon J. Myatt, and John D. Gregg to meet with Seymour S. Berlin, the director of the Bureau of Executive Manpower in the Civil Service Commission. A summary of that meeting is contained in the following letter I sent to Congressman Dulski on March 1, 1971:

<u>*PERSONAL AND UNOFFICIAL*</u>

Honorable Thaddeus J. Dulski
United States Court House
Niagara Square
Buffalo, New York 14202

Dear Thad:

Pursuant to the instructions contained in your letter of January 15, 1971, our Committee had the privilege of meeting with Mr. Seymour S. Berlin, Director, Bureau of Executive Manpower, Civil Service Commission.

Mr. Berlin was most cordial and cooperative, and extended to our Committee every courtesy. We discussed our recommendations with him and Mr. Wilson Matthews, Director, Office of Hearing Examiners. After our discussion, it appeared that our recommendations would properly fall within the purview of Mr. Phillip N. Oliver, Director of the Job Evaluation and Pay Review Task Force, who has already forwarded to our attention his draft notes, relative to Hearing Examiners, for evaluation and comment.

Our Committee has prepared for Mr. Oliver's consideration an analysis of the Hearing Examiner position, and I hope that further exchanges of views will result in a mutually satisfactory resolution of the matter.

On my next trip to Washington, I look forward to seeing you and thanking you personally for your interest and assistance in this matter.

Sincerely,
/s/ Frank
Frank B Borowiec

Cc: Mr. Seymour S. Berlin
    Director, Bureau of
    Executive Manpower
    US Civil Service Commission
    Washington DC

We thought it important that, in pursuit of a new position title, our association get some exposure before a congressional committee. Thanks to the good offices of Congressman Dulski, Harry B. Kallman, a member of our association's executive committee, and I, as president, were asked to appear before the House of Representatives Subcommittee on Employee Benefits on June 13, 1972, to give testimony on proposals submitted by the Job Evaluation and Pay Review Task Forces.

If the Association of Hearing Examiners was to be judged by the company it keeps, it would have had a sky-high rating at that congressional hearing. The names and affiliations of the other witnesses summoned to testify at that hearing on federal job evaluation and pay illustrate that assertion:

- Dr. Jerry O'Callaghan, national president of the Federal Professional Association
- Mr. Paul F. Robbins, executive director of the National Society of Professional Engineers
- Mr. John F. Lipton, president of the Professional Air Traffic Controllers Organization

The hearing was scheduled before Representative James M. Hanley, chairman of the subcommittee. Harry Kallman and I submitted our association's position documents for the record. We were the first to give testimony. The hearing went extraordinarily well, and Harry and I believed that it augured well for the future of our enterprise.

The postage, time, and travel expenses incurred in giving testimony on behalf of the hearing examiner corps before the House and Senate committees and in attending our joint committee meetings with the Civil Service Commission and with representatives of the Federal Trial Examiners Conference was having a most deleterious effect on our association's treasury. I therefore asked the executive board to have our members vote on an amendment to our constitution to approve a raise in our annual dues from four dollars to twenty-five dollars. It passed overwhelmingly, 121 to 18.

On August 15, 1972, I received the following letter from Congressman T. J. Dulski, who had been my elected representative:

Mr. Frank B Borowiec
Suite 487
795 Peachtree Street
Atlanta, Georgia, 30308

I have just received a call from the office of Chairman Hampton, US Civil Service Commission, advising that the tile of Hearing Examiner will be changed to "Administrative Law Judge."

I am sure you will be pleased to learn of this action.

With kindest regards,

> *Sincerely yours,*
> */s/ Thad*
> *T. J. Dulski*

On August 23, 1972, Congressman Dulski forwarded to me a copy of a letter dated August 18, 1972, that he had received from Robert E. Hampton, chairman of the Civil Service Commission:

Honorable T. J. Dulski
Chairman, Committee on Post Office
*   and Civil Service*
House of Representatives
Washington, DC 20515
Dear Mr. Chairman:

This has reference to your letter of May 2, 1972, concerning the class title of the position of Hearing Examiner.

The Commission has carefully reviewed this matter. It has considered the views of the officials in many regulatory agencies, Hearing Examiners, members of the Judiciary, bar associations and other groups and individuals having an interest in the field of administrative law.

I am pleased to advise you that on the basis of its study the Commission has decided to amend Part 930 of its regulations and change the title of the position from Hearing Examiner to Administrative Law Judge.

> *Sincerely yours,*
> */s/ Bob*
> *Robert E. Hampton*
> *Chairman*

In gratitude for their support of our efforts to secure a proper title for the corps of hearing examiners, (now administrative law judges), I sent the following letters to Congressman T. J. Dulski and Mitchel F. Mazuca, district director of the United Steelworkers of America.

September 5, 1972

The Honorable T. J. Dulski
House of Representatives
Washington, DC 20515

Dear Thad:

"A friend in need is a friend indeed."

Thanks to your encouragement and support, our efforts to secure a meaningful change of title from the Civil Service Commission have resulted in success.

The Social Security Administration has established and maintained a traditional high standard of service to the public, and has provided the citizens of this country the protection of "due process" guaranteed to them by our laws and the Constitution. Your action will ensure to the aged and disabled wage earners of this country a system of justice that will continue to provide for them a high level of competence and expertise.

The type of leadership you have displayed in this most important matter will soon make the Bureau of Hearings and Appeals of the Social Security Administration a model in the area of Administrative Law and the public interest will thus be better served.

With kindest personal regards, I remain,

Sincerely yours,
/s/ Frank
Frank B Borowiec
Administrative Law Judge

Mr. Mitchel F. Mazuca, District Director
United Steelworkers of America
300 Edwards Building
155 Franklin Street
Buffalo, New York 14202

Dear Mike:

Thanks to your assistance and support, the title of "Judge" has become a reality.

It is gratifying that with all of your other problems, you could find the time to actively assist me in securing a change in title. Your steadfast belief that the change in title was important in order for the Social Security Administration to maintain its traditionally high standards of service to the public and at the same time ensure to the aged and disabled wage earners of this country a system of justice that will provide a high level of competence and expertise is most commendable.

Your most able efforts to protect the rights of the wage earners and taxpayers of this country merit the praise and appreciation of all citizens.

With kindest personal regards and thanks, I remain,

Sincerely yours,
/s/ Frank
Frank B Borowiec
Administrative Law Judge in Charge

On January 12, 1973, as president of our association, I mailed to Charles J. Dullea, the director of the Office of Administrative Law Judges in the Civil Service Commission, the original and copies of a resolution passed by the governors of our association, which recognized *"their wisdom, foresight and courage in creating the new uniform title … in furtherance of equal justice for all citizens of the United States who have relations with their government in the field of Administrative Law."*

The one epistle that still, two and a half decades later, fills me with a sense of pride and joy was the "Newsletter from the President" that I sent to all the judges on November 10, 1972:

It is with a deep sense of pride that I address each of you as "Administrative Law Judge." So many people have worked so hard and so long to make the title a reality that it still is a little difficult to believe that the former title of "Hearing Examiner" is no more."

                              s/s   Frank B Borowiec

As one writer opined, "The title of Administrative Law Judge added a sense of decorum and propriety that enhanced the legitimacy of an agency's dealing with the public."[10]

Amen!

---

10   D. Cofer, *Judges, Bureaucrats, and the Question of Independence: A Study of the Social Security Hearing Process* (1985). Greenwood Press, Westport, Connecticut.

REGIONAL CHIEF
ADMINISTRATIVE LAW JUDGE

The battle for a new title was over, and I was exhausted. The burden of my duties as the administrative law judge in charge of the Atlanta office, the responsibilities of representing the best interests of administrative law judges as the president of their association, and my family obligations as a husband and father of four growing teenagers made my decision not to run for a third term as president an easy one.

In my farewell letter of June 28, 1974, I took great pride that during my tenure as president we were able to accomplish the following:

- Increase our paid membership
- Secure a change in title to "Administrative Law Judge"
- Reduce the backlog by volunteering to hear additional cases in Appalachia and the Great Lakes area
- Adopt a new constitution
- Adopt a canons of ethics, which reduced to writing those principles that should govern the personal conduct of the members of the administrative judiciary
- Raised annual dues from $4.00 to $25.00

I looked forward to resuming a more normal lifestyle, but Dame Fortune had other plans for my future.

I had barely started to relax when I received a call from Dale Cook. He wanted to appoint me as the regional chief judge for Region IV of the Bureau of Hearings and Appeals. Region IV was the largest region in the country, encompassing the states of Georgia, Alabama, Florida, Mississippi, Tennessee, South Carolina, North Carolina, and Kentucky.

There must be some gene in my DNA that does not permit me to say no to any new assignment or challenge. I, of course, accepted the appointment as the regional chief administrative law judge effective June 30, 1974. Happily, the appointment did not require any move on my part, as the regional office was only two blocks from the hearing office.

The regional chief administrative law judge is the professional and administrative head of the Social Security Administration's Hearings and Appeals program for one of the ten Social Security Administration regions. The incumbent has overall responsibility for planning, directing, and coordinating the total program within the region. The incumbent would attend quarterly meetings of the regional chief judges scheduled by the director in Arlington, Virginia.

My appointment was well received by the judges in the region, partly based on my efforts in securing the new job title. As the regional chief judge, I made it a point to visit and acquaint myself with the personnel in all of the hearing offices. In a region that large, communication on a personal basis was important, so to minimize my travel, I formed the Regional Judicial Council, which consisted of fifteen judges. Specifically, every judge in charge of an individual office was a member, and to add some variety and spice to our monthly meetings, we invited on a rotating basis five judges who were not a part of management to attend our monthly meetings. This proved to be very popular with the regular judges who were not a part of management. The hope of being selected one of the five to attend the bimonthly meeting was a great morale booster. In selecting the five judges, we made it a point to always include some naysayers. This gave greater validity to our bimonthly meetings, and any changes we initiated were immediately carried back to the hearing office by the judge in charge for implementation. The decisions of our council, because of the transparency of our meetings and the fact there had been input from the rank and file, were quickly and easily put into place in the entire region. Strangely, and counterintuitively, the presence of the naysayers resulted in greater harmony, and any motions made were always unanimously carried.

At the national level, working with our director, Dale Cook, and the other regional chief judges was a joy. There were of course many problems to be solved on an ongoing basis, but we readily accepted the challenge.

The most pressing problem was that on a national basis our case receipts suddenly began to rise at an alarming rate when in 1972 Congress enacted the Supplemental Security Insurance Program,[11] which extended benefits to individuals who were disabled but had no relevant work history and who had not contributed to the trust fund. These payments would be made from general tax revenues but would be administered by the Social Security Administration. Congress also enacted the black lung disability program for disabled coal miners. The addition of these two new programs resulted in a deluge of new cases, which meant that the time from when a claimant requested a hearing to the actual hearing was over two years.

---

11   Social Security Amendments of 1973, Public Law No. 92–603.

The long delays severely impacted the lives of the claimants, who wrote their congressional representatives that they did not have the financial resources to wait two years or longer for a hearing. Congress looked to the Social Security Administration to address the delays that so adversely affected their constituents.

The federal judiciary also became involved in the failure of the system to provide timely justice for disabled claimants. See *Caswell v. Califano* (435 F. Supp. 127) and *White v. Matthews* (559 F. Supp. 852). These decisions and others would order the immediate payment of Social Security cash benefits ninety to one hundred twenty days after a request for a hearing. The eventual hearing for the individual claimant would only address the issue of whether the benefits should be terminated if the claimant was found not to be disabled. This seemed to be eminently fair to the courts, since more than 50 percent of all claimants were found to be disabled at their hearings.

It should be noted, however, that the fact that a majority of the cases denied at the initial levels were being reversed by the judges in the Bureau of Hearings and Appeals was a source of continuing embarrassment to the Social Security Administration officials. In their internal memos circulated within the agency, they rightly or wrongly believed that their decisions were 90 percent correct. I had always believed that if the agency's initial decisions were accurate and correct, the Bureau of Hearings reversal rate should hover around 10 percent.

One administrative law judge reported the following after attending a class for newly hired judges: "On my second day as an Administrative Law Judge, my 'class' was addressed by Rhoda Greenberg, then Director of the Office of Disability Programs. In her remarks she informed us that the State Agencies were correct 95 percent of the time. I, along with many other judges felt that this was, in effect, a statement that most claims deserved to be denied …"

BUREAU OF HEARINGS
AND APPEALS
CAUGHT BETWEEN A ROCK
AND A HARD PLACE

As a consequence of these backlogs, H. Dale Cook, the director of the Bureau of Hearings and Appeals, was caught in the crosshairs of the Department of Health Education and Welfare, Congress, the courts, and the Social Security Administration.

At his meetings with the regional chief judges, he urged us to alert all administrative law judges of the urgent need for greater productivity. We assured the director that we and the judges in our regions were well aware of the burgeoning backlog and the catastrophic effects it was having on the claimants who were appearing before them, and of course we would do all within our powers to reduce the backlog.

To that end, in January of 1973, in an attempt to decrease the backlog, fulfill our obligation as public servants, and bring earlier hearings to those individuals who were caught up in the backlog, we asked for volunteers who would take an additional docket of cases in the Great Lakes area, where the largest backlog existed. The response of the judges to "Operation Rescue" was overwhelmingly favorable, and judges from coast to coast requested the assignment of these additional cases. Within days, we had the disposition of more than four thousand cases guaranteed by voluntary assignments.

We were shocked to discover that the regional office managers issued instructions that no travel orders would be issued to volunteers from their region. As managers, they viewed our efforts as an unauthorized and improper usurpation of their prerogatives and responsibilities. They believed that our efforts made them look bad.

H. Dale Cook's and the regional chief judge's attempts to provide hearings expeditiously was also made difficult, if not impossible, by the simple fact that the bureau had been historically underfunded in terms of providing additional staff and resources to provide the due process hearings required by the Administrative Procedures Act. Specifically, the Bureau of Hearings and Appeals had eight hundred vacancies at a time when the backlog was approaching one hundred thousand cases. One has to speculate why no other bureau in the Social Security Administration was similarly treated. Some writers have opined that this was an attempt by SSA to rid itself of the Administrative Procedures Act by establishing that its use in Social Security hearings was in and of itself the cause of the backlog.

Thanks to the efforts of H. Dale Cook, these agency attempts to weaken Administrative Procedures Act protections were effectively frustrated. As noted earlier, prior to his appointment as the director of the Bureau of Hearings and Appeals, Cook had important political connections. He had served as the first assistant U S attorney in Oklahoma City and as legal counsel and advisor to Governor and later Senator Henry Bellmon and had played a role in Richard M. Nixon's 1968 presidential campaign. Dale Cook's political ties to Congress and the administration were strong enough to shield him and the bureau from any adverse agency action.

The significance of his political stature was all the more evident when on January 17, 1973, even though the case backlogs were still a significant problem, he was awarded the Secretary's Special Citation by HEW Secretary Elliott Richardson in recognition of his outstanding leadership to the corps of administrative law judges and as the managerial director to the Bureau of Hearings and Appeals.

The judge's and the bureau's sheltered status under Dale Cook's protective mantle abruptly ended when in 1974 he was appointed the US district judge for the Northern, Eastern, and Western Districts in his beloved state of Oklahoma. He served with distinction on the federal bench for thirty-three years until his death on September 22, 2008. In recognition of his unfailing dedication to the law, the federal building and the US Courthouse in Tulsa, Oklahoma, were renamed the H. Dale Cook Federal Building and United States Courthouse.

I will never forget that at our final meeting in Washington DC, before he left for Oklahoma, he called me aside, and with sadness in his voice said, "Frank, I am sorry to tell you this, but it looks like the bureau is in for a rough future. The new people do not seem to have the same concerns about the rule of law that you and I have shared."

His concern for the future was most prescient.

THE BACKLOG

As the backlog increased, the thousands of claimants who were awaiting a hearing for a year or more besieged their congressional representatives with pleas to intervene on their behalf. The members of Congress were overwhelmed by more than three hundred thousand letters from their constituents demanding action. A majority of their staff's time was devoted to Social Security issues.

When Commissioner James B. Cardwell appeared before the Senate's Commission on Aging, he was asked by Senator Edward M. Kennedy, "What are we supposed to do ... tell our constituents they are going to have to wait eleven months, two years, or more? I don't think we can go back now and tell the people to be a little more patient when they are desperate right now."

When questioned by the senator, Commissioner Cardwell admitted that an estimated twenty thousand Social Security recipients fail to receive their checks each month. "If a check does not come for a month, it is not a minor inconvenience—it is a disaster," said Senator Kennedy, who chaired that committee hearing.[12]

---

12 Hearing before the US Senate, Special Committee on Aging (Future Directions in Social Security) (March 20, 1975).

I was not the only one who had observed that the high rates of reversal by ALJs might be indicative of a failure of the initial decisions at the state level.

At the Senate Committee on Aging, Senator Lawton Chiles had the following exchange with SSA Commissioner James B. Cardwell:

Senator Chiles: More than 50 percent reversals; that would seem to indicate that in the preliminary investigation ... there is something wrong. With a 50 percent reversal rate, it would seem to indicate ... that the job is not being done in the earlier stages.

Mr. Cardwell: You have struck a nerve; you have really struck a very lively nerve in the whole matter of the disability process ... All I can say is that I have asked the same question that you asked: Is there not something wrong? And I think the answer is probably "yes" ...

Senator Chiles: I think it would just have to be "yes" if you got more than 50 percent ... I have the feeling that in any kind of judicial system ... if you are having 50 percent reversals, you are going to do something about your lower court judges, or you are going to take them to school. You are going to say, "You are being reversed half of the time."

So what are you doing about using these reversals as a means of educating your hearing officers and hearing personnel?

Mr. Cardwell: I would like Mr. Crouch ... to speak to that question. That is a good question ...

Mr. Crouch: (testifies)

Senator Chiles: Well, I still did not quite get an answer to my question.

Mr. Cardwell: (a) very high reversal rate seems to be fundamental to the program, whether it is 50 percent or whatever. It has something to do, I believe, with the process. (Hearing before the US Senate, Special Committee on Aging, March 20, 1975.)

Senator William S. Cohen in his remarks[13] to Congress took a more direct and less kindly assessment of the high reversal rates of the state agencies: "The message perceived by the State Agencies was to deny, deny, deny ..."

Clyde M. Weber, representing the American Federation of Government Employees, AFL-CIO, described the plight of the aged, blind, and handicapped individuals suffering from the delays in having their claims processed. In analyzing the problem, he testified:[14]

The grievousness of the situation is manifest ... yet the solution really is rather simple. The problem does not lie in defining the analysis or prescribing the remedy. The problem lies simply and solely in the bureaucratic strategies of ... the Department of Health, Education, and Welfare, which imposes inertia and frustration on the Social Security Administration.

Almost all the difficulties in the implementation of the Supplemental Security Income program derive from the impingements interposed by HEW ... on the Social Security Administration.... The Department of Health, Education, and Welfare has pursued a consistent policy of "disincentive" in the matter of an efficient and rapid accomplishment of the goals enunciated in the Social Security Amendments of 1972....

It is germane to realize that the present secretary of the Department of Health, Education, and Welfare ... is imbued with the philosophy ... *to give precedence to money matters over the rights of human beings.*

---

13   See 130 Cong. Rec. S6213 (May 22, 1984).

14   Hearing before the US Senate, Special Committee on Aging (Future Directions in Social Security) .

This new approach by the DHEW was not without its critics at the highest levels of management. Robert J. Myers, an actuary, helped to create the Social Security program when he was asked by President Franklin D. Roosevelt in 1934 to serve on a panel that was drawing up blueprints for America's first comprehensive social insurance program. The program had to be self-supporting, financed principally by payroll taxes. One of the principal problems he faced was determining at what age individuals could stop working and begin drawing benefits. His initial calculations, based on actuarial data, indicated that the correct age should be sixty-seven, which would ensure that the system would be solvent. When the Social Security Act was signed into law in 1935, the age had been lowered to sixty-five.

"Why is it sixty-five? Why not?" Myers wrote in a 1992 memoir, *Within the System: My Half Century in Social Security.* "That age has been credited to … or blamed on … German Chancellor Otto von Bismarck. In truth, he didn't do it."

Bismarck, in fact, selected seventy as the minimum qualifying age when he established the world's first social security system in 1889.

"Age sixty-five was picked because sixty was too young and seventy was too old," Myers wrote. "So we split the difference."

His name and career are inseparable from the history of Social Security. It is most significant that, as an actuary, he fully understood the implications of Social Security's *new policy of giving money matters precedence over the rights of individuals. He wrote that this threatened to "steer Social Security down a dangerous unsound financial course."* As a matter of conscience, he resigned his position and left his beloved creation, the Social Security Administration.

His talents and expertise, however, were so remarkable that various federal agencies and congressional panels retained his services as a consultant. The depth of his abilities is best demonstrated by the fact that in 1982 President Ronald R. Reagan asked him to return to government service as the deputy commissioner of the Social Security Administration.

In 1983, as a matter of conscience, he again resigned his position with the Social Security Administration citing "disastrous" meddling by the Office of Management and Budget, which had proposed changes that Myers thought would penalize the poor.

Why had the Social Security Administration strayed so far from its mission, that even its most loyal and dedicated personnel could not in good conscience want to be identified with it?

Did Senator Cohen, in his remarks to the Congress, perceive the situation correctly when he stated that the Social Security Administration was sending the following message:[15] *"Deny, deny, deny ..."*

The backlog escalated exponentially at the Bureau of Hearings and Appeals (BHA), while incomprehensively, backlogs did not exist anywhere else in the Social Security system. Management meetings were scheduled between SSA and BHA to address the issue. In my naïveté, the solution seemed obvious. BHA was being flooded by thousands of cases that were being denied at the initial state agency level. BHA was reversing more than 50 percent of their decisions.

It is important to recall that in 1935, to gain passage of the Social Security Act, a tradeoff took place in the Congress where, the individual states, and *not* the Social Security Administration, were assigned the duty of making the initial disability determinations. The state operations

---

15   See 130 Cong. Rec. S6213 (May 22, 1984).

would be fully funded by the Social Security Administration, but strangely, their disability decisions would *not* be based on the Social Security law and regulations but on a manual that attempts to interpret the Social Security law and regulations.

Thus, to initiate a Social Security disability claim, an individual will go a local Social Security district office to complete an application and any associated forms. The district office will forward the claim to the state Disability Determination Service (DDS), where an adjudicator will review all pertinent disability factors and issue an "initial decision." This decision is based solely upon the jurisdictional and medical evidence of record. The adjudicator never sees or meets the claimant.

The manual used at the state level is the Program Operations Manual System (POMS), and it is the basis for the initial Social Security disability decisions which on appeal are reviewed by the Administrative Law Judges and the Federal Courts.

Unfortunately for the Social Security Administration, the administrative law judges and the federal courts cannot legally rely on or cite the POMS manual, which is considered a secondary source; they must rely on the actual language of the Social Security Act and the Social Security regulations as a basis for their decisions.

Two different standards—and even more egregious, the ALJs and the courts, in reviewing the initial Social Security disability decisions, cannot base their decisions on any POMS material on which the Social Security Administration may have relied in issuing its initial decisions.

Might this fact explain the basis for the extraordinary difference in the decisions reached by each group? Duh.

It seemed incongruous and a little strange to me that the Social Security Administration would permit the use of two different criteria for judging the facts in the same case at separate levels of adjudication, that is, at the state agency level and at the ALJ level.

I proposed that SSA abandon or rewrite the POMS for its field personnel so that it would reflect and track more closely the Social Security Act and the Social Security regulations. I surmised that if the SSA field personnel and the ALJs were using the same playbook, the numbers of cases appealed to BHA would dramatically decrease very rapidly. Problem solved!

I was quickly brought back to the "real world." A senior official explained the weakness and flaw in my solution: money! I will take the liberty of paraphrasing his remarks ...

"Borowiec, if we adopted your solution, it would cost the Social Security Administration $60 billion dollars[16].... The existing system costs the Social Security Administration $50 billion dollars[16] ... because a lot of people do not appeal their disability denials ... the budget allocated to BHA to manage all the appeals is $1 billion dollars[16].... By continuing the existing system, SSA saves $9 billion dollars[16] ... case closed!"

His assessment of the budgetary situation is well supported by the statistical data.[17]

---

16 Numbers used are for illustrative purposes. I have no current memory of the exact figures quoted at that time.

17 Improving the Social Security Administration's Hearing Process, Hal Daub, Chairman, (September 2006). Social Security Administration, Baltimore, Maryland.

"Of all the claims filed in 2000 … 40 percent were allowed at the state agency level; 4 percent were allowed at the reconsideration level; 38 percent denied by the state agency did not pursue their claim to the hearing level. The remaining 18 percent did pursue their claim to the hearing level or beyond, of which two-thirds were eventually allowed and one third denied."

This dual standard still continues.

THE AGENCY SOLUTION

T hus a collision was inevitable between the independent, unbiased, and impartial judges sworn to protect the due process interests of individual claimants to a fair hearing free of agency influence and the agency managers directed to resolve a troubling national backlog.

The Social Security Administration managers, still unhappy and institutionally embarrassed by the ongoing high reversal rates of their disability procedures, then seized upon the backlog as an opportunity to resolve this glaring defect in their program. Their solution was quite simple. They needed a scapegoat. Blame these high reversal rates on "judicial error" by the administrative law judges.

They overlooked the obvious statistical data[18] that showed a high degree of correlation between the numbers of favorable hearing decisions issued by hearing offices in states with high initial allowance rates and those in states with low allowance rates. Over a twenty-year interval, 1985 to 2005, the low allowance rate states' unfavorable decisions were reversed 80 to 90 percent of the time by ALJs, while the high allowance states were reversed only 40 to 60 percent in that time frame.

---

18 Ibid.

The median allowance rate for the median judge for the middle range of state agencies was relatively stable between 69 and 71 percent.

To an unbiased observer, it would appear that there was more consistency in the decisions of the administrative law judges than in the state agency decisions they reviewed on appeal over a two-decade period.

Dennis R. Fox, who had been employed by both a state agency and the Social Security Administration, reviewed the disability program in a *Journal of Social Behavior and Personality*[19] article.

The inadequacy of the process is demonstrated by the fact that more than 60 percent of claimants denied by DDSs successfully appeal. Discussions with DDS and SSA workers in several parts of the country revealed that these problems were widespread, a situation confirmed by the General Accounting Office (1986). SSA itself noted that widely disparate allowance rates and the high proportion of incorrect denials quickly escalated (Office of Assessment, 1987). SSA is under constant judicial pressure to liberalize standards and procedures according to legal concepts rather than medical or bureaucratic ones. The agency traditionally resists such efforts, preferring instead its own interpretation of legislative mandates.

Fox observed that "if the states and ALJs continue to use essentially different standards of judgment," that is, the law and regulations by one and POMS by the other, then SSA's approach of providing more training, more guidelines, and more supervision while ignoring "the concept of impairment itself" will never resolve the backlog and allowance issues.

---

19 Dennis R. Fox, "Observations on Disability Evaluation in the Social Security Administration," *Journal of Social Behavior and Personality*, 9, 237–246 (1994).

A further reason for the disparity between DDS and ALJ decisions is that the ALJ actually sees, observes, and questions the claimant. "This allows a focus on the individual's subjective experience rather than on the 'average person' approach of the formal rules," writes Fox.

It was astounding to him that the standard for allowance differed so dramatically between the DDS and the ALJ decisions. DDS, he observed, may allow a claim only if it is 95 percent "medically certain" that the underlying impairment fully causes the inability to work; the judge may award benefits if a *preponderance,* or 50.1 percent, of the evidence shows that the impairment is a *contributing* cause.

The report "Improving the Social Security Administration's Hearing Process"[20] concluded, "This growth in backlogs and in waiting times that would accompany it is not inevitable." It recommended three ways to avoid that:

1. Increase resources spent on the hearing process.
2. Reduce the flow of cases into the hearing process.
3. Increase production levels.

The agency, however, came up with a novel, if not legally supportable initiative. To speed up the process and productivity, the agency proposed to dispense with all those "due process" trappings and "fair and just hearing" procedures that lawyers and judges love to discuss in court and in decisions.

This position was articulated by the commissioner of the Social Security Administration, James B. Cardwell, who stated that the "Social Security Administration's Bureau of Hearings and Appeals is

---

20 Improving the Social Security Administration's Hearing Process, Hal Daub, Chairman.

hurt by the unnecessary trappings of the Administrative Law Judge system.... I would like to eliminate the ALJ concept from SSA and use hearing officers instead."[21]

The Social Security Administration, therefore, proposed that the administrative law judges be removed from the protections Congress provided in the Administrative Procedures Act. If the judges were not under that protective umbrella, the backlog could be eliminated by establishing production quotas for each judge, mandating what percentage of cases a judge could favorably rule on, establishing mechanical procedures for deciding a case free of input from the denied claimant, and so forth. Thus, SSA in its publications and public relations releases began to "spin" the situation to its advantage by fixing the blame for the backlog and delays in the hearing process on judicial error and the Administrative Procedures Act.

The great tragedy in this type of statement and solution from the executive in charge of the Social Security Administration is that it attempted to undermine the integrity of the Bureau of Hearings and Appeals. It is unfortunate that this agency would expend such great effort to deprive the citizens and taxpayers of this great nation of their constitutional right to a fair and impartial hearing.

In addressing the questioned accuracy of administrative law judge decisions, one judge opined:

"The ALJs live in a fishbowl! Our hearings are recorded. Our decisions are written and subjected to the Appeal Council's review and appeal by the claimant. An increasing number of claimants are represented by an attorney. There is District Court review. There are

---

21   D. Cofer, *Judges, Bureaucrats, and the Question of Independence: A Study of the Social Security Hearing Process* [1985], Page 70.

Civil Service and departmental rules on hours and conduct and an enforcement system. If this isn't accountability, what is?"

To implement the agency position, a program was put in place to target any judge who ruled favorably in more than 45 percent of the cases on his docket. The judge would be subject to immediate agency review. This proposal was made in spite of the fact that the appealed decisions of every judge are in the ordinary course of business reviewed by the federal district court judges, the Circuit Courts of Appeals, and the US Supreme Court. A random reading of the decisions issued by these courts of appeal might lead the reader to believe that, if anything, the administrative law judges might be too conservative in deciding their cases.

Since the Social Security Disability Amendments of 1980[22] required the Social Security Appeals Council to review administrative law judge decisions granting benefits, administration officials interpreted that language as authorization to amend or reverse the judges' favorable decisions administratively, all in support of their core belief that a high rate of favorable decisions was a fortiori indicative of administrative law judge error. This assumption, in retrospect, was an attempt to save face and had no factual or statistical basis.

This ill-conceived strategy by Social Security Administration executives to reduce or explain the burgeoning backlog by targeting administrative law judges with high allowance rates produced an endless stream of litigation by aggrieved claimants and administrative law judges and—most embarrassing—an ever increasing number of court decisions denouncing these Social Security Administration policies.

The agency's solution could not paper over an "inconvenient truth" referred to by Senator Lawton Chiles in his questioning of Commissioner

---

22   Public Law No. 96-265 § 304(g), 94 Stat. 441, 456 (1980).

Cardwell when he appeared before the US Senate's Special Committee on Aging.

"More than 50 percent reversals," Chiles said. "That would seem to indicate that in the preliminary investigation ... there is something wrong. With a 50 percent reversal rate, it would seem to indicate ... that the job is not being done in the earlier stages."

Commissioner Cardwell failed to take advantage of this opportunity to address the "reversal problem" by explaining to the senator that the Social Security Administration does not make the initial determination on a disability application. That to gain passage of the Social Security Act, a trade-off took place in the Congress, whereby the individual states were assigned the duty of making the initial disability determinations. The Social Security Administration in its administration of the disability program adopted the Program Operations Manual System (POMS) to be used by all of its employees when processing disability claims. The state operations would be fully funded by the SSA, and their disability decisions would be governed by the POMS manual.

The commissioner, in further explanation, could have testified that variations quickly arose among the states on the rates at which benefits have been paid or denied and that there were inconsistencies in the states' disability decisions and the amount of resources made available to the state agencies to fund their disability programs. He could have explained that the POMS, while intended to clarify and interpret the complexities of the Social Security Disability Program, contains multiple provisions that are in direct conflict with the law, the regulations, and federal court decisions. It would have been important to inform the senator that the administrative law judges (ALJs), the US District Courts, the Circuit Courts of Appeals, and the US Supreme Court are all bound by the Social Security Act and the SSA regulations in reaching any decision in a disability claim. The ALJ and the courts cannot rely on POMS or cite or reference POMS in any decision that they issue, since that manual has no legal standing or validity. Therefore, the reason for the high reversal rates by the ALJs is simply that ALJs and the state DDSs use different standards to decide disability cases!

This would have been a more responsive answer to the senator's inquiry, and this admission would certainly have explained the high reversal rate, but not his failure to revise the POMS so that it would be in accord with the law and the regulations.

Instead of the above, the commissioner testified that "a very high reversal rate seems to be fundamental to the program, whether it is 50 percent or whatever. It has something to do, I believe, with the process."

"AN AGENCY AT WAR WITH ITSELF"

The Social Security Administration is one of the nation's most successful legislative achievements. In one way or another, Social Security affects the lives of almost every American family.

The program collects contributions from more than one hundred million workers, covers nearly two hundred million Americans, and disburses $4.3 billion a month in cash benefits. To thirty million beneficiaries ... one out of every seven Americans. Almost 100 percent of all people sixty-five or older are eligible for Social Security benefits, as are men and women aged 21–64 in the event a family breadwinner incurred a severe long-term disability. Ninety-five percent of mothers with dependent children are eligible for benefits if the father of the family dies.

For older Americans, the Social Security program is the foundation on which their economic security rests. Social Security benefits represent more than half the income of two-thirds of aged single beneficiaries and one-half of elderly couple beneficiaries. They account for almost the total income of nearly one-third of the single elderly beneficiaries and 15 percent of older couples.[23]

---

23 US Senate Special Committee on Aging, March 20, 1975, Statement of Clyde M. Weber, representing the American Federation of Government Employees, AFL-CIO.

I t is one government agency that truly enjoys the confidence and trust of the American people.

The secret of its great success is that SSA has truly mastered the economy of scale. This invaluable standardization enables SSA to efficiently and routinely handle millions of retirement and disability claims.

Unfortunately, SSA's attempts to impose these macro procedures on its Bureau of Hearings and Appeals brought another microeconomic phenomenon, "diseconomy of scale," into play.

As noted earlier, deciding the presence of a "disability" under the Social Security law is the most elusive and complicated determination ever devised by man in any judicial or quasi-judicial legal system. In reaching a decision in an individual case, the administrative law judge must combine elements of medicine, subjective complaints of pain, existence of work, and the uniqueness of the individual claimant. A finding of disability is thus a quasi-legal conclusion, a quasi-medical decision, and a quasi-sociological theory or possibly a quasi-philosophical premise.

The SSA desperately needed a magic bullet that would allow for a simple and rapid resolution of the massive backlog in Social Security disability cases. SSA sought to categorize all of the above-cited factors in a disability decision and give each factor a numerical value. Then, if a claim scored at or above an assigned level that defined disabled, benefits would be automatically awarded to that claimant. Voila! Problem solved and the backlog disappears.

It soon discovered that no such magic bullet exists. A disability claim, because of its very nature, does not lend itself to such mass adjudication, as each decision must be tailored to the individual claimant. The only magic bullet to reduce the number of appeals of its initial decisions would be to modify the POMS to clearly reflect the law and the regulations. This approach, as noted earlier, for cost reasons was rejected.

Further, there are additional stumbling blocks in evaluating a claim using mechanical standards where pain, depression, and physical limitations are present. If a claimant has both psychological and orthopedic disabilities, what weight should be given to the physical and emotional impairments to constitute the *substantial* evidence required to support a favorable finding of disability, which again, as noted earlier has never been well defined. The US Supreme Court attempted to do so in the case of *Consolidated Edison Co. v. NLRB (305 U.S. 197)* when it defined *substantial* evidence as "more than a mere scintilla. It means such relevant evidence as a reasonable mind might accept as adequate to support a conclusion,…" evidence that rational individuals would normally rely upon in conducting their daily affairs.

How do you, or can you, introduce economy of scale concepts into a legalistic hearing system where the above rules and hearing requirements are so ill defined? It was and still is an irresolvable problem for the Social Security Administration and not susceptible to resolution by simplistic agency regulations.

The very forces that give the Social Security Administration its enviable reputation for effective use of economies of scale were difficult if not impossible to apply to its Bureau of Hearings and Appeals because of its focus on the individual.

As noted earlier, in my own instance, when operational problems presented themselves, the small size of the Bureau of Hearings and Appeals (BHA) gave it the unique flexibility to rapidly clarify and resolve a local program's problems. If I had been required to request a resolution from the Social Security Administration as to which jobs were light or sedentary and so forth in the Atlanta, Georgia, area, it would literally have taken months for Social Security to research the "problem" and propose a solution, and who can estimate how many more months to determine if the proposed solution actually worked. Economies of scale are in the field of individual disability adjudication generally a disincentive.

The Bureau of Hearings and Appeals is a minuscule part of the Social Security Administration. If one can imagine a large hot water tank as representing the Social Security Administration routinely containing millions of cases, the Bureau of Hearings and Appeals represents the tiny pressure relief valve that takes over for the Social Security Administration to review and resolve those difficult, pesky, and unusual cases that fall outside the norm. Because of its unique position, BHA is well suited to quickly and fairly resolve that small percentage of disability cases that unresolved would put extreme pressures on the Social Security Administration. BHA was never intended to do the mass adjudication of hearing claims *incorrectly* decided by the state agencies—*incorrect* only in the sense that they were using a different and inapplicable legal standard. The optimal use of the BHA would be to limit its jurisdiction to reviewing only those cases where all of the parties had used the same songbook.

Why the Social Security Administration persists in attempting to put these small numbers of difficult cases back into the tank is perplexing. It can be compared to putting the proverbial square peg into the round hole!

In explaining the role of the Bureau of Hearing Appeals in the rubric of the Social Security Administration, I compared it to a manufacturing plant producing widgets. If I am the manager of that plant and I observe that 50 percent of my widgets are being rejected by my inspectors on the final inspection line, I would instruct my foremen to review our procedures to learn why there are so many rejections and make the necessary corrections to reduce the number of rejections. The managers of the Social Security Administration adopted another solution—fire the inspectors!

This SSA solution to control the Bureau of Hearings and Appeals by disregarding the mandates of the Administrative Procedures Act led to what many commentators have described as the era when the agency was at war with itself.

The irony of the situation is that both antagonists, in good faith, truly believed that their processes would best serve the disabled claimants: one relying on the Administrative Procedure Act, and the other on agency and administrative initiatives and techniques.

The battle lines were drawn for the inevitable confrontation!

ROBERT L. TRACHTENBERG

In January of 1975, James B. Cardwell, the commissioner of the Social Security Administration, appointed Robert L. Trachtenberg to head the Bureau of Hearings and Appeals.

On paper it was an excellent selection by the commissioner.

Bob Trachtenberg was, by profession, a lawyer, so he was well familiar with the intricacies of the Administrative Procedures Act, a skill that would serve him well as the director of the bureau. Further, he had exemplary credentials as a manager who could recognize and immediately address any problems associated with the backlog and the bureau's high reversal rates of its subordinate components.

More important, as he entered on his duties to provide some kind of managerial direction to the Bureau of Hearings and Appeals, he knew that any actions he proposed would be fully backed and funded by the SSA and the DHEW.

What could go wrong?

In a nutshell, illegitimate and intrusive micromanagement of BHA's administrative law judges outside the parameters of the Administrative

Procedures Act by the Social Security Administration and the Department of Health, Education, and Welfare.

Well, as Dale Cook prophesied as he left BHA to accept his federal judgeship, "The new people do not seem to have the same concerns about the rule of law that you and I have shared." This lack of concern by the Social Security Administration, unfortunately, was coupled with a biased and distorted view of their Corps of Administrative Law Judges.

Mr. Trachtenberg, however, in a meeting with DHEW Secretary Joseph Califano on January 6, 1978, in describing the administrative law judges that he supervised, expressed a contrary view:[24] "that we have an exemplary group of Administrative Law Judges, that they are not, quote, fat cats, close quotes, that their level of output is now at the maximum, that there has been more than a hundred percent increase in productivity over the last three years, that the quality of decisions has not suffered."

At that same meeting with Mr. Califano, in response to a question by the secretary as to how the Social Security Administration officials viewed its Bureau of Hearings and Appeals, he advised the secretary that some people in the Office of General Counsel and at the Baltimore home office of the Social Security Administration had a totally opposite view and perceived the Bureau of Hearings and Appeals and its administrative law judges as follows: [25]

"There are more than six hundred uncontrolled, unmanaged, and unsupervised employees at a very high level ... that's an Administrative

---

24   *Weaver v. Califano*, U.S.D.C. No. C76-1437A, deposition of Frank B Borowiec, 02/15/1978; p. 20.

25   Ibid., pp.21-22.

*Law Judge ... who cannot be managed in traditional terms." So he says,
"I don't say this to frighten you, but it is a real concern as to how you get a
handle on the judges and manage them in traditional terms."*
  Q. Those were Mr. Trachtenberg's words?
  A. Yes, sir."

As the regional chief judge for Region IV, the largest of the nation's
ten regions, I, and the other regional chief judges, of course, met early
on with Bob Trachtenberg and his management team. I was fully
aware of Dale Cook's assessment of his successors, but in my twenty
years as counsel for the Steelworkers Union, I had many opportunities
to deal with managers of all stripes and colors. In this instance, I was
an integral part of a new management team, and I was committed to
making Bob Trachtenberg's agenda to make BHA more effective a
reality. Fortunately, I found Mr. Trachtenberg to be knowledgeable and
reasonable in his approach to the backlog problems, but I suspected he
was getting a lot of pressure from "Baltimore."

Still, I believed that the future looked promising.

His initial proposals as he articulated them were quite modest:[26] "I
was set on making two fundamental decisions," he said. "One, take the
ALJs out of non-judicial functions, and two, reduce the backlog."

Two immediate initiatives pressed by Mr. Trachtenberg, which all of
the chiefs cheered, were additional funding for the bureau and the filling
of over eight hundred position vacancies. Because of the underfunding,
there was a severe shortage of staff, so many ALJs had been compelled
to perform clerical duties just to move their cases along.

---

26 *Federal Times*, April 26, 1978.

A management team was put in place to make these goals a reality, and sadly, as many cynics have observed, the devil is in the details. My alarm bells began to ring when I discovered that this management team was not staffed by BHA people but by Baltimore headquarters people. Further, and more disturbing, it appeared that their chain of command on an organizational level would be more closely linked to Mr. Cardwell than Bob Trachtenberg.

The management team submitted a report written by Assistant Bureau Director for Administration John L. Poore for Mr. Trachtenberg to introduce and enforce. The regional chiefs suddenly became aware that Mr. Trachtenberg's appointment came with a great many strings attached in the form of the independent authority given by Baltimore to Mr. Trachtenberg's assistant, John Poore. It appeared that Mr. Poore had his own back door power base in SSA's central office in Baltimore. Technically, on the organization chart, he appeared as the "assistant" bureau director reporting to Mr. Trachtenberg, but in actuality he also reported to Baltimore. This made the other regional chief judges and me uncomfortable. I am sure that it must also have had a similar effect on Mr. Trachtenberg.

John Poore's management team recognized that it would not be able to carve out a congressional exemption from the Administrative Procedures Act, but it concluded that under the guise of new and enhanced management techniques and initiatives, to ostensibly reduce the expanding number of backlogged cases, it might regain agency control over the ALJs in the Bureau of Hearings and Appeals. The management team concluded that it could use the ever-increasing backlog as prima facie evidence that, because of the requirements in the Administrative Procedures Act, it was impossible for the Social Security Administration to carry out its mission to provide timely hearings for aggrieved claimants.

The following initiatives by the management team were then informally presented to the regional chief judges over a period of time as a fait accompli!

1. A quality assurance program to identify ALJs who had high numbers of allowances
2. A model hearing office "reconfiguration." A new position of hearing office administrator was to be created who would manage the hearing office and who would not report to the regional chief administrative law judge, but rather directly to his or her superiors in the Bureau of Hearings and Appeals Central Office in Arlington, Virginia. The rationale for this initiative was to free the administrative law judge from his onerous administrative duties so that he could hear more cases.
3. The creation of a "vocational grid" to make disability determinations in a standardized manner without the need for any input from the disabled person as to the specific nature of his or her disabilities.
4. Creation of production "goals," not "quotas," for all administrative law judges
5. A peer review program
6. Attendance at the National Judicial College in Reno, Nevada, as an award for "superior accomplishment" under the Government Employees Incentive Act
7. Removal of administrative law judges who failed to meet production goals

Initially, as presented, each initiative except for the last four, which were never publicly disclosed, could fairly fall, if judiciously administered, within Bob Trachtenberg's expressed goals for the Bureau.

The good news was that for the first time in more than a decade, not only were the eight hundred vacancies filled, but additional clerical workers were hired to deal with the backlog. More significant was the hiring of hundreds of recent law school graduates who were assigned to work with individual judges.

This hiring of additional staff brought immediate positive results in both case dispositions and backlog reductions. At one of the earlier regional chiefs' meetings, Bob Trachtenberg's management team then introduced a formula for success in attaining the goals Trachtenberg had set for himself. Statisticians believed that if the judges, who were now fully staffed, could dispose of on average twenty-six cases per month, the backlog would be a thing of the past. The judges, now fully staffed, quickly responded and within a year the backlog was reduced to ninety thousand cases, as the statisticians predicted, and was receding at the rate of twenty-five hundred cases per month. Commissioner Cardwell wrote a memo to the judges thanking them for meeting the challenge.

Unfortunately for the Bureau of Hearings and Appeals, Commissioner Cardwell never acted on the need to revise the POMS, so we were all following the same guidelines. As a result, soon after Commissioner Cardwell's congratulatory letter, at a meeting of the regional chiefs, Director Trachtenberg announced that his well-laid plans had been "foiled" by the state agencies when they increased their number of denials, which resulted in a staggering 25 percent increase in our case receipts. This was most disruptive of his well-thought-out plans for reducing the backlog.

I recalled his frustration in my deposition[27] of February 17, 1978.

---

27   *Weaver v. Califano*, p.73.

Q. Did Mr. Trachtenberg, at your January meeting of this year, discuss any of these factors?

A. Yes, he did. He made mention of the fact that he was very pleased; he asked for about twelve thousand cases per month, which we had been doing. Suddenly ... I will read you his exact language on this. He says, "A year ago, we were almost current. Then the state agencies did it to us again. We were not able to control our destiny, so the bottom line is that they just swamped us with more requests for hearing." So where he had initially predicted ... that by issuing twelve thousand decisions per month, we would be current, he suddenly found that to be current required the issuance of eighteen thousand cases a month.

The management team, the statisticians, and Commissioner Cardwell had all acknowledged that by reaching the twenty-six decision goal set by Mr. Trachtenberg, the fully staffed ALJs were handling their dockets with optimal efficiency. The bottom line was that the expected goal of twenty-six cases a month would no longer reduce the backlog. As a result, the backlog quickly climbed back to the same levels present when he assumed the office of director.

Stronger measures to increase productivity were needed. The pressure was on Bob Trachtenberg to do something, and do it quickly.

He was given no credit for his initial success in reducing the backlog. Forces beyond his control now dominated the BHA landscape. In any event, Robert L. Trachtenberg had proven that he was a capable manager. He had taken the ALJs out of many of their non-judicial functions and had initially reduced the case backlog.

I was never able to speak directly to Bob Trachtenberg as to the origins of these management initiatives submitted by Mr. Poore, but I always felt that if given a little freer rein, his management approach to these issues would have been far different. He would instinctively have recognized that the administrative law judge was a peculiar brand of federal creature. The administrative law judge's independence was grounded in statute to insulate him from external pressure. Bob would have used the "velvet glove" approach as compared to the "iron fist" approach of Mr. Poore's management team.

As a regional chief, I was proud of the judges and their staffs in my region who had responded so ably in meeting a goal of twenty-six cases per month. I did my best to advance Bob Trachtenberg's goals to improve the position of the judges while reducing the backlog. My problems focused on the John Poore management team's decision to take over the duties of the regional chiefs and the judges in charge of individual offices. His clumsy attempts to reduce our status to that of a potted plant I usually was able to circumvent by delay or by some other management ploy. Through the use of my Judicial Council, I made sure that the management operations officers he had installed in every hearing office were always subject to the authority of the judge in charge of that office.

On every occasion that presented itself where the Poore management team had overstepped its bounds, I readily took that opportunity to publicly exploit their operational errors if they in any way threatened the decisional independence of my judges. It was not the type of mission I took any pride in. I was a part of the management team, and as such, I believed that it demanded my loyalty to the organization of which I was a part. Through all of 1975 this cat-and-mouse game between me and the Poore management team continued unabated. I proved to be a thorn in the side of his management team's efforts to control the hearing offices. I had to be removed as the regional chief of the nation's largest and most productive region.

This conflict came to a head in April of 1976 at a meeting of the regional chief judges. Again from my deposition of February 15, 1978:[28]

Q. If I understand you correctly, the administrative functions of transfer, travel, leave, have all been transferred?

A. What happened, in one meeting I can remember, we had a judge transferred in from Manchester, New Hampshire, and he came into the Atlanta office and he called me and said he had no staff. And I attempted to get him some staff so that he would be gainfully employed, since the government and taxpayers were paying him a salary. I had no results, you know, in just the normal procedures. So at a meeting in Washington, I brought this to the attention of the Division of Administration at a formal meeting of the Regional Chiefs. The ... my problem was that I felt under my job description I should be able to assign personnel to that judge that he may stay busy. It was a comedy of errors. They said, "Our computers still show him to be in Manchester, New Hampshire." Of course, as I pointed out, those computers were in error. The man was actually in Atlanta begging for work. I was told that that was no longer my function that ... who needs staff and what numbers would be handled by the Division of Administration.

Q. Who told you that?

A. That was told by Director Trachtenberg. He said, "If there is any question, then you want to appeal, then you feel free to come to me and indicate where you feel that you have been aggrieved by the decision." At that point, there was no sense pursuing it ...

Q. Did you have any other conversations during that meeting which dealt with this kind of problem, the fact that you no longer had the authority to make, provide support staff?

A. Yes, sir.

Q. Who did you have the conversation with?

---

28   Ibid., p.20.

A. *In the course of a general business meeting with all the Regional Chiefs. They became, as you might imagine, angry because I felt, I believed, I had a duty, responsibility as the Regional Chief Judge to the Judges to be sure not only did they work but that they had a quality product. In effect, I was told that that was no longer my concern, that I was not a manager and they were experts in management and they would concern themselves with these matters. Eventually, one of the gentlemen jumped up on my table. It was a funny affair ... and waved his finger at me. He became angry with the fact that I wanted to enforce my job description.*

Q. *Who was that that jumped up on the table?*

A. *It was Mr. John Poore.*

Q. *What did he say when he jumped up on the table?*

A. *He said, "I am bigger than you are now, Judge Borowiec," and I said, "I am sure you are." From there it was downhill. I just felt I really was going nowhere. And rather than turn over these duties to others ... I didn't feel my duties as Regional Chief basically could be delegated to a non-lawyer, to a non-judge. I felt I was appointed only because of my prior legal and judicial experience. I didn't feel I could delegate this to a third party because the job description said ... again, I make reference to it ... indicates that I was responsible to see that the Civil Service requirements and regulations pertaining to administrative law are met. I felt that under these kinds of circumstances, I could not function effectively and I resigned in May of 1976 ... I didn't want to sign my name to a paper for an action which I had not been responsible for ... They were in charge. And being a good team player, I just quietly folded my tent and stole away.*

On April 15, 1976, I dispatched the following letter to Robert L. Trachtenberg:

Mr. Robert L. Trachtenberg, Director
Bureau of Hearings and Appeals, SSA
Post Office Box 2518
Washington DC 20013

Dear Mr. Trachtenberg:

Since June 30, 1974, I have had the great honor of serving as the Regional Chief Administrative Law Judge for the Social Security Administration in the Southeastern Region of the United States.

Under my stewardship, I believe that the Bureau of Hearings and Appeals in this Region has prospered and the following represents a brief summary of my activities as the Regional Chief Administrative Law Judge for Region IV:

1. *The Judges' productivity in this Region has increased significantly almost double that of June 1974.*
2. *New direction and purpose has been instilled in the regional Administrative Law Judge Corps to recognize and meet Bureau problems.*
3. *The judges have now whittled down our regional backlog to approximately seventeen thousand cases, which approximates one hundred cases per judge. Our goal of processing cases on a ninety-day cycle should be reached in the immediate short term.*
4. *The Black Lung caseload in Region IV will be disposed of by April 30, 1976, except for those few cases awaiting development and new requests for hearing.*
5. *The Development Center is now current and the informal remand process is doing well.*
6. *The creation of a Regional Judicial Council has been a highly effective instrument in disseminating information and maintaining high morale.*

7.   *The inauguration of a regional program to improve relations with the other operating bureaus will enhance the Regional Bureau of Hearings and Appeals' image at both the Regional and Field Office levels, and more important, provides an effective vehicle to solve common problems informally and expeditiously.*

8.   *The formation and implementation of the "Case Profile Project" in this region brought about significant improvements in recognizing and disposing of cases which did not require a formal hearing.*

The above programs and innovative procedures have been implemented in spite of the fact that additional Regional staff positions were not made available by the Regional Personnel Office. A permanent staff of ten individuals has been responsible for staffing, space, and equipment needs for twenty-seven offices and more than seven hundred professional employees. This is a real credit to their dedication and enthusiasm to reach our common goals of providing the public with the highest quality of justice, in the shortest period of time and at the least possible cost.

The administrative supervision of a Region as large as Region IV (eight states, twenty-seven offices, more than seven hundred people) is truly a most demanding task and leaves only little time for the hearing and deciding of cases, which of course is an integral part of my job description and the principal mission of this Bureau.

The administrative experience has been rewarding, but because peer leadership and direction are time-consuming, it is my suggestion that this administrative experience should be shared by other judges over a similar two-year tour of duty.

Therefore, I request that I be granted permission to return to the performance of my judicial responsibilities as an Administrative Law Judge in the Atlanta, Georgia, Bureau of Hearings and Appeals Field Office. Upon your approval of my reassignment as an Administrative Law Judge in the Atlanta Bureau Hearings and Appeals Field Office, I could then formally submit my resignation as the Regional Chief Administrative Law Judge. Pending the approval of my reassignment to the Atlanta Bureau of Hearings and Appeals Field Office, I will, of course, be most pleased to continue with my current duties so that a continuity of leadership may be assured.

Your early and favorable consideration, approval, and implementation of the above request is as always much appreciated.

> *Sincerely,*
> */s/ Frank B Borowiec*
> *Frank B Borowiec*
> *Regional Chief*
> *Administrative Law Judge*

On April 27, 1976, I received the following response to my reassignment request from Director Trachtenberg:

Frank B Borowiec, Regional Chief
> *Administrative Law Judge*
Room 641
50 Seventh Street, N.E.
Atlanta, Georgia 30323

Dear Frank:

On the occasion of your stepping down as the Regional Chief Administrative Law Judge for Region IV, I would be remiss if I failed to acknowledge my appreciation for your performance in that position over the past fifteen months.

Needless to say, your unselfish action in resigning is in the absolute best interest of BHA and is in keeping with your dedication to bettering the Bureau and its ALJs. It is important to me that you know that your decision in this matter will in no way alter my regard for you as an individual nor will it diminish my expectation that you will continue in a leadership role within the Bureau. Indeed, I hope that I can continue to seek your counsel on the many key issues facing the Bureau.

I also want you to know that I have come to consider you a friend over the past many months, and I would want nothing to change this relationship.

Thank you again for your contributions and untiring efforts in helping the Bureau reach its present level of accomplishment.

> *Sincerely,*
> */s/ Bob*
> *Robert L. Trachtenberg*
> *Director*

I am sorry to report that I did not receive a similar letter of friendship from Mr. John L. Poore.

On April 23, 1976, I sent a memorandum to all personnel in Region IV enclosing a copy of my request for reassignment.

On June 28, 1978, true to his hope "that I can continue to seek your counsel on the many key issues facing the Bureau," Bob Trachtenberg requested that I serve on an ALJ National Policy Council modeled after my own Judicial Council in Region IV. Its goals would be the same, to seek "early input on important policy issues" and to "open lines of communication with the Field and Central Office." He noted that "the principals I am asking to sit on the ALJ National Judicial Council hold strong views and do not have the reputation of 'yes' persons."

"You are being asked to serve because of your demonstrated interest in improving BHA administrative justice and because you hold a view and perspective which I should consider in developing Bureau policy."

Unfortunately, I was then serving on the American Bar Association Executive Committee's Judicial Administration Division for its Conference of Administrative Law Judges, and on July 5, 1978, I wrote the following letter to Director Trachtenberg:

Dear Bob:

Thank you for your most gracious invitation to serve ... I have, however, committed myself rather heavily to certain American Bar Association activities and do not feel that I would be able to give the Council position the time and effort it requires. I therefore must respectfully decline at this time until I have fulfilled my preexisting commitments to those other professional programs.

/s/ Frank

I did not fully comprehend how well our Judicial Council had kept the judges in Region IV informed of my attempts as regional chief to deflect, delay, or ignore those management initiatives proposed by BHA's Division of Management that were in conflict with the Administrative Procedures Act. The mail I received from the judges in Region IV immediately after I submitted my letter of resignation was totally unexpected.

The following are excerpts from the numerous letters I received, which are a reflection of the sentiments of the rank-and-file administrative law judges to the "administrative" changes proposed by BHA's Office of Administration.

"I would like to briefly express my appreciation for the manner in which you have so diligently carried out your demanding, and, I am sure, exasperating duties as Regional Chief Judge. Having been granted the opportunity to attend the last Judicial Council meeting, I could not fail to be impressed by the various pressures that have been placed upon you and the excellent job you have done in articulating the interests of the amorphous mass of ALJs in the field."

"It is regretted that Region IV and all of BHA is losing your outstanding leadership at such a crucial time, although all of us realize we can count on your continued support. It has been a source of confidence to have served as an ALJ with you."

"It has been such a gratifying experience for us to work with you that we would like very much for you to stay in your Regional Chief Law Judge position."

"Thank you for all of your valiant efforts on behalf of the Field!"

"I take genuine pride in writing you and extending my sincere congratulations for a job well done in yeomanly fashion in the momentous and, oft times, thankless position of Regional Chief Administrative Law Judge. With your innovations and the achievements and progress accomplished by the Region under your leadership, you have etched a place for yourself in the annals of history in BHA."

"I feel a sense of sadness because my good friend will no longer preside over the region and I will not hear the same friendly voice when I pick up the telephone to discuss a problem. I also have a feeling of pride in your achievements, particularly the whittling down of the case backlog ... and a little pride for my own small part in helping you to accomplish these important goals. It goes without saying that I will miss you at the helm!"

The single event that made my efforts on behalf of the judges in Region IV so priceless and invaluable and that characterized the strong professional bond that existed between us was the following resolution they enacted:

RESOLUTION
Be it Resolved by The Regional Judicial Council
For
Region IV, Bureau of Hearings and Appeals
Meeting, August 3, 1976, in Atlanta, Georgia , that:
Honorable Frank B Borowiec
Served with great fidelity and distinguished leadership
as
Regional Chief Administrative Law Judge
GHA, Region IV, Atlanta, Georgia

Judge Borowiec by his courageous and independent-leadership of the corps of Administrative Law Judges of Region IV, BHS-SSA-HEW, liquidated an unusual backlog of cases thrust upon the Bureau by two new claims programs passed by Congress and increased the efficient processing of Social Security Claims in the largest region in the United States.

Judge Borowiec was always faithful to the Congressional mission of the Bureau, which is to serve the people of the United States by moving Social Security Claims appeals rapidly, efficiently and fairly. At the same time Judge Borowiec never ceased to protect the independence of the Judges under the Administrative Procedures Act, which was enacted by the Congress to protect the people of the United States from arbitrary agency decisions and to insure due process of law to claimants in administrative matters.

This resolution is voted, August 3, 1976, as a testimony of appreciation from the corps of administrative law judges who stood with him for independent administrative justice for the people of the United States.

It is further voted that this Resolution be engrossed and presented to Judge Borowiec.

The passage and presentation of this singular award was especially meaningful and significant to me because such resolutions and awards are usually a function and province of management. In my case, it came from the hearts of my fellow judges.

All these humbling letters and awards to a "damn Yankee" in the heart of "Dixie."

THE BATTLE FOR DUE PROCESS
AND THE RULE OF LAW

~~~~

With the passage of time, I have come to believe that my resignation as regional chief judge was, at best, the opening musket shot for the oncoming administrative law judges' struggle to preserve the rule of law in the Bureau of Hearings and Appeals (BHA).

On a more sober note, the judges in Region VII, situated in Kansas City, Missouri, had not fared as well with their regional chief judge and BHA's Office of Administration. As a sign of their discomfiture, they fired a cannon shot across the bow of BHA and the Social Security Administration.

The attacks on their judicial independence had become so egregious that their only recourse was to file a lawsuit. On November 16, 1977, Administrative Law Judges Charles N. Bono, William W. Cochrane, Edward L. Jandt, Henry G. Reese, and Hammond C. Woods filed suit[29] in the US District Court for the Western District of Missouri against the Social Security Administration; the Bureau of Hearings and Appeals; James B. Cardwell, commissioner of the SSA; Robert L. Trachtenberg,

---

29   *Bono, et al. v. United States of America, Social Security Administration, et.al.*, No. 77-0819-CV-W-4 (W.D. Mo.).

director of the Bureau of Hearings and Appeals; Phillip T. Brown, chief administrative law judge, Bureau of Hearings and Appeals; and Myron D. Mills, regional chief administrative law judge, Region VII.

In their complaint, they cite the applicable provisions of the Administrative Act and pertinent regulations, the BHA handbook, and the ALJ position description and conclude by alleging the following:

Defendant BHA and defendants Mills, Brown, and Trachtenberg, in their official capacities as administrative officials of BHA, have promulgated various regulations, orders, directives, memoranda, and instructions that are invalid on their face and/or as implemented for one or more of the following reasons:

    a) They violate the constitutional guarantee of Social Security claimants to procedural due process, under the Fifth Amendment.

    b) They violate or are contrary to the statutes, regulations, and directives governing the administration of the Social Security Act.

    c) They exceed the statutory authority of BHA and its administrative officials.

    d) They violate prior governing regulations adopted by the BHA.

    e) They violate the statutes and regulations governing the powers, authority, responsibilities, and duties of the plaintiffs and of all ALJs similarly situated.

Their complaint then makes specific reference to various administrative actions relative to "scheduling the place of hearing for specific cases; denying approval of scheduled out of town dockets; requiring a production of twenty-six cases per ALJ within a reporting period; threatening to transfer ALJs who fail to meet this quota …"

Specifically, they alleged that establishing and implementing the "Regional Office Peer Review Program" violated the intent of the Administrative Procedures Act in that it singled out for review specific ALJs to control their performance and to establish illegal production criteria. Paragraph 24 of their complaint alleged that,

- *Defendant Mills has knowingly and willfully misused his administrative powers as RCALJ to:...*
- *Pressure plaintiffs and other ALJs similarly situated to meet quantitative quotas of case dispositions.*
- *Assign or withhold assignment of staff personnel to individual ALJs without regard to their workloads so as to impair the performance of their duties and for the purpose of improperly punishing those ALJs who met with his disfavor.*
- *Threaten transfer or removal of ALJs and closing of hearing offices to compel meeting of arbitrary quotas.*

They asked the court "to issue a declaratory judgment holding that the regulations, orders, directives, memoranda, instructions, and practices ... are invalid; that they conflict with those statutes and regulations providing for the independence of ALJs free of agency control and influence; and that they are arbitrary and capricious."

The filing of this lawsuit should give the reader some small sense of the bitterness, distrust, and downright anger present in the Corps of Administrative Law Judges that they were compelled to sue their own government and agency to correct a flagrant abuse of their administrative authority.

The Social Security Administration and the Bureau of Hearings and Appeals quickly recognized the weakness of their legal position and the futility of proceeding to trial. On June 7, 1979, a settlement was reached.

The settlement conceded the authority of management to exercise administrative and management oversight over the ALJ corps but expressly provided that management would not issue any memoranda setting a specific number of dispositions by ALJs; case assignments to ALJs would be rotated; travel policies were revised so that travel was under the control of the ALJ; productivity of an individual ALJ was not to be used as a criterion for approving transfer applications and the Bureau's Peer Review Program and Quality Assurance Program were to be used only for providing data to management to facilitate its internal operations.

The settlement thus eliminated overt production pressures by management, but as some writers[30] have opined, it "provided little protection for the original ALJ concerns."

The ALJs, however, believed that the negotiated settlement was in the best interests of both parties and they had no reason to doubt the good faith of management. Yet forces beyond the control of both parties were to negate the ALJs' initial attempt to establish a long-term dialogue with BHA.

---

30 Cofer, *Judges, Bureaucrats, and the Question of Independence,* Page 116.

A POLITICAL INTERLUDE

B efore the filing of the lawsuit[31] by the Kansas City five, an intervening political event had occurred. In November of 1976, the country had elected a Democratic president. Until that moment, my only viable political ally had been Congressman Thad Dulski. The executive branch and by definition all government bureaus had been under the control of the Republican Party. Fortunately, Dale Cook, who had been active in President Nixon's campaigns, believed in the rule of law and under his aegis, BHA was relatively safe from bureaucratic incursions.

With his appointment to a federal judgeship, it was apparent we had no ally in the upper echelons of management. The election of Jimmy Carter meant that the ALJs had an opportunity to fill a major executive branch position in DHEW to replace the voice of our lost leader, Dale Cook.

The ALJs came up with a wild, impossible plan that might help to maintain their decisional independence under the Administrative Procedures Act: place an ALJ in the highest echelons of the new administration. This would give us a voice and a seat at the table or tables that would deal with the backlog and agency attempts to limit the constitutional rights of citizens seeking access to a full and fair hearing.

---

31   *Bono, et al. v. United States of America, Social Security Administration.*

Based on some of my earlier political successes, I was asked by the Corps of ALJs to seek appointment as the general counsel of the Department of Health, Education, and Welfare.

That same gene in my DNA that does not permit me to say no to any new assignment or challenge reappeared, and I accepted the challenge. I realistically assessed our chances of securing the appointment as slim, at best. Almost a decade had almost passed since I left the political arena in Buffalo, New York, and other than my friends, the Steelworkers and some major Polish American fraternal organizations, my contacts in the US Senate and the House of Representatives were almost nonexistent.

I had seriously underestimated the political muscle that was present in our corps of administrative law judges. Almost overnight I began receiving copies of letters to and acknowledgements from members of the House and Senate from Hawaii to Maryland, Texas to North Dakota, all urging President-elect Jimmy Carter to appoint me as the general counsel for DHEW.

The ALJs in Texas contacted the Speaker of the House of Representatives, Carl Albert, recommending that the office of general counsel of DHEW "be filled by the most honorable, capable, and knowledgeable attorney in the nation. Frank B Borowiec is a lawyer of highest quality who has demonstrated his eminent qualification for appointment as General Counsel of the Department of Health, Education and Welfare."

The Texas ALJs did not stop with writing a letter on my behalf. They arranged a meeting with Speaker Albert's staff, which resulted in my receiving the following letter from the Speaker:

The Speaker's Rooms
U.S. House of Representatives
Washington DC 20515
December 2, 1976

"Thank you for dropping by ... when you were in Washington earlier this week. Thanks, too, for your letter. We have been pleased to write the President-elect on your behalf ... We feel you would do an excellent job as General Counsel of the Department of Health, Education and Welfare."
Sincerely,
/s/ Carl Albert
The Speaker

From across the Pacific Ocean from the Aloha state of Hawaii came a most unexpected and welcome endorsement for the position of general counsel in DHEW addressed to Senator Daniel K. Inouye.

"Big Frank," as I call him, was the hearing officer in charge of the Hearing Office in Atlanta, Georgia, to which I was originally assigned. He was real nice to me ... I developed such an impressive image of him that I was moved a few years ago to urge that he be given a more important role in our government to make it a healthier establishment. So much for my impertinent intermeddling. Happy New Year to you and the family.

From my home state of New York, Congressman Henry J. Nowak wrote me.

I regret that I was not here to welcome you to Washington, but I do hope everything works out so you will be here permanently. You appear to be a natural for the position of General Counsel with the Department of Health, Education, and Welfare, and I am more than pleased to recommend you to President Carter.

On December 12, 1976, President Jimmy Carter replied to Congressman Nowak.

I appreciate your high regard for Judge Frank B Borowiec, and assure you that I will give every consideration that he serve as General Counsel of HEW.
Sincerely
/s/ Jimmy
Jimmy Carter

I had no personal recollection of knowing anyone on Staten Island, New York, yet one of my fellow ALJs forwarded a letter to me sent by Joseph P. Delaney, the Staten Island coordinator for the NY Citizens for Carter to the Carter/Mondale Planning Group.

I am proud to recommend Mr. Borowiec for your consideration.... An individual of Mr. Borowiec's proven ability would certainly indicate that the candidate who asked "why not the best" has chosen the best!

Would you believe I really actually had a personal contact on Staten Island, my daughter Deborah? It was Mr. Delaney who refreshed my recollection. In his letter of endorsement, he noted the following:

During the campaign, I had the pleasure to meet Mr. Borowiec. His daughter Debby was a very active Carter supporter on Staten Island and an invaluable member of our campaign staff. I was impressed by Mr. Borowiec's integrity and experience.

What an amazing coincidence that my daughter would play such a significant role in my quest for the position of general counsel!

A letter to Congressman Carroll Hubbard of Kentucky included the following:

"He has been and is the strongest advocate of protecting the rights of all individuals insured under the Social Security Act. He believes their claims should be protected and adjudicated pursuant to the Administrative Procedures Act so as to provide prompt, full, impartial, and independent hearings and decisions. He has the full confidence and support for this very important position by all of the Administrative Law Judges I know."

Congressman Hubbard was kind enough to send a letter on my behalf to President Carter. He wrote the following:

In 1975, he personally led a team of judges into Lexington, Kentucky, to alleviate the badly congested docket. When relieved by the present administration in May of 1976, there was no longer a backlog of cases in the IVth Region.

Thanks to the efforts of the Corps of Administrative Law Judges, similar letters of endorsement flooded our ad hoc campaign committee. Congressmen and senators from Texas, Kentucky, New York, Mississippi, Maryland, Hawaii, Illinois, Georgia, California, Wisconsin—from the rocky coasts of Maine and Oregon and from the Gulf to the Canadian border—sent their letters of recommendation to the Carter/Mondale Planning Group.

It was a heady and exhilarating feeling to be back in the political arena. This was all the more enhanced when I began receiving letters requesting that, upon my appointment, I consider employing the writer in my department. Surely, this was a good omen and indicative that our efforts would be met with success.

What could go wrong?

We underestimated the genius of the opposition. We were cleverly outmaneuvered. Management made the position of general counsel a career civil-service position outside the domain of the Carter/Mondale Planning Group. Our research clearly showed that this position was not in the competitive civil service, but our protestations fell on deaf ears. As my friends in the Steelworkers who had actively supported my candidacy communicated to me, "Labor generally has not carried much weight with the present administration." The same can be said of the corps of administrative law judges.

President Aloysius A. Mazewski of the Polish American Congress and the Polish National Alliance was very much upset by this turn of events, and on March 16, 1978, he sent the following letter to the President Carter.

Mr. President,

Our Community is very disappointed in the lack of response of your administration for a meeting ...

You have spoken to many of us prior to the election ... wherein you said, "you can count on full participation of Americans of Polish descent in my administration." ... Our community supported you and relied on it.

To the contrary, we have not made gains. The first day after your inauguration, you replaced Leonard Walentynowicz and Mitchell Kobelinski.

If you would have replaced them with Americans of Polish descent, we would not have felt hurt, but to discharge them without any indication of other appointments is disappointing.

Just recently, an outstanding public servant in HEW, serving in Atlanta, Georgia, Frank B Borowiec, whose qualifications and experience are of the highest, sought the position of General Counsel at HEW. He had the support of the leadership of the Democratic Party, and now we find he was ignored, not even considered, and someone else was appointed. This also adds to our concern over the seriousness of your statement ...

Respectively yours,

/s/ Aloysius A. Mazewski

THE END OF THE TRACHTENBERG ERA

~~~~~~~~

1975–1979

In 1979, Bob Trachtenberg, frustrated in his efforts to effectively manage the Bureau of Hearings and Appeals, took advantage of the change in administrations to resign his position as director.

As the director of BHA, he had to be included as a defendant in the slew of lawsuits that resulted from management attempts to do the following:

- Set a specific number of dispositions by ALJs
- Control the rotation of case assignments and travel policies of ALJs
- Use productivity as a criterion for approving transfers for an individual ALJ
- Illegally house review ALJ decisions
- Target judges who issued too many favorable decisions

As a result, he was spending inordinate amounts of time attempting to defend the Bureau of Hearings and Appeals, rather than pursuing the goals he had set for himself when he assumed the office of director: to take the ALJs out of non-judicial functions and reduce the backlog.[32]

In defining Robert Trachtenberg's tenure, Commissioner Cardwell stated,[33] "He is a lawyer, he has a passion for serving people. And he's tough. And Bob turned the screws on the ALJs. Sometimes he was too hard, and he may have turned the screws too tight. But he believes they ought to be supervised. And he definitely wants to sort out the non-performers."

It is interesting to note that when Bob Trachtenberg first assumed the directorship of the BHA, he had a less kindly view of the bureau.[34] He viewed his new charges as "the most lethargic, indifferent, unresponsive, and unaccountable organization that I have ever seen in fifteen years as a Federal employee."

Mr. Trachtenberg's harsh view softened in time as can be perceived from his meeting with DHEW Secretary Joseph Califano on January 6, 1978. In describing the administrative law judges he opined[35] "that we have an exemplary group of Administrative Law Judges, that they are not, quote, fat cats, close quotes, that their level of output is now at the maximum, that there has been more than a 100 percent increase in productivity over the last three years, and that the quality of decisions has not suffered."

In 1979, he did recognize that his attempts to implement some initiatives had only generated "rancor, distrust and, indeed, poor morale among the ALJs."

---

32 *Federal Times*, April 26, 1978.

33 Cofer, *Judges, Bureaucrats, and the Question of Independence*. Page 75

34 *Weaver v. Califano*, U.S.D.C. No. C76-1437A, deposition of Frank B Borowiec, 02/15/1978. Page 21.

35 *Federal Times*, 1978.

But, in defense of these initiatives, he added, "It continues to be my view, however, that as Bureau Director, my first responsibility is to serve Social Security claimants—not the ALJs."

I think the poem, "The Job," author unknown, best describes the reasons for Bob Trachtenberg's resignation:

I'm not allowed to run the train.
The whistle I can't blow.
I'm not the one who designates
how fast the train will go.
I'm not allowed to blow the steam
or even ring the bell.
But let the damn thing jump the track
and see who catches hell.

FROM BAD TO WORSE

After his departure, tragically, the Bono settlement, which relied on the good faith of both parties, was effectively dismantled.

At a Senate hearing, Mr. Louis B. Hays (Mr. Trachtenberg's successor) denied that the agency had put improper pressures on the judges.[36] "No attempt is ever made to influence the outcome of a particular case," he said. "There is not now and never has been a goal or quota established for acceptable allowance or denial rates."

He was contradicted by Senator William S. Cohen, who said he had obtained an internal memorandum from the Social Security agency setting a goal for each judge to dispose of forty-five cases a month.[37] The document, he noted, stated that Social Security officials would take "appropriate adverse actions against underachieving administrative law judges."

The record now shows that Senator Cohen was correct, in that Mr. Hays, in 1981, had, in fact, set a goal of forty-five dispositions a month.

---

36 D. Cofer, *Judges, Bureaucrats, and the Question of Independence*, 147.
37 Ibid., 140.

The failure of Jimmy Carter to win reelection brought in a new team to head DHEW that was not kindly disposed to the concepts embodied in the Administrative Procedures Act.

DHEW, the Department of Health, Education, and Welfare, in 1979, became the Department of Health and Human Services, HHS.

The new administration announced a goal of cutting $3.4 billion in disability costs during its first term in office. To accomplish this, position papers were prepared alleging that 20 percent of the individuals receiving disability benefits were not disabled. To eliminate one out of every five disabled persons from the disabled rolls would come close to saving the $3.4 billion figure. It appeared to many cynics that the $3.4 billion figure was arrived at by establishing the actuarial value of the average disability claim and then determining what percentage of those individuals' benefits totaled $3.4 billion. It was quicker and simpler than a prolonged, detailed statistical analysis of actual cases. If you were one out of the five selected for a cessation of benefits,… well … good luck in fighting the agency's subjective decision to stop your disability payments.

The administration's lobbying, coupled with its strategy and position papers, worked remarkably well. In 1980, pursuant to these initiatives, Congress directed that all disabled persons would be required to prove once every three years that their disability was continuing. As frosting on the cake, Congress responded to the agency's long-term goals to gain greater control over the Corps of Administrative Law Judges by passing the infamous "Bellmon Amendment."

A report prepared by the US Senate Subcommittee on oversight of Government Management of the Committee on Governmental Affairs some years later, in September of 1983, gives us a revealing insight as to how the Social Security Administration "planted" certain initiatives in the Senate bill that would circumvent some of the restrictions imposed on its appeals process by the Administrative Procedures Act.

As noted in the following excerpt from the report of the subcommittee, administration officials used the language favorable to their cause in the Senate bill, which had been stripped from the legislation by the conference committee, to initiate a program that would legally allow them to intimidate those judges who found favorably for a litigant in more than 50 percent of cases. All in support of an agenda to strip $3.4 billion from the disability budget.

According to the report, "In 1980, Senator Henry Bellmon sponsored an amendment to the Social Security Amendments of that year which provided the following:

"(g) The Secretary of Health and Human Services shall implement a program of reviewing, on his own motion, *decisions* rendered by administrative law judges as a result of hearings under section 221(d) of the Social Security Act, and shall report to the Congress by January 1, 1982, on his progress." (Emphasis added.)

There is very little legislative history on the Bellmon Amendment. It was offered as an unprinted floor amendment by Senator Long on behalf of Senator Bellmon, who simply introduced the amendment and submitted the written statement of Senator Bellmon for the record. The amendment was accepted by the Senate without debate.

According to Senator Bellmon's statement, the SSA was to review the allowance decisions of those ALJs with high allowance rates. In addition, as passed by the Senate, the amendment not only required the Secretary of HHS to report to Congress on the progress of the program, but outlined what was to be considered and included in the report:

"In his report, the Secretary must indicate the percentage of decisions being reviewed and describe the criteria for selecting decisions to be reviewed and the reversal rate for individual administrative law judges by the Secretary (through the Appeals Council or otherwise), and the reversal rate of State agency determinations by individual administrative law judges."

However, when the amendment was taken up for review by the conference committee, the committee struck all language specifying what was to be included in the report to Congress. Thus, the conference committee struck all references to the assessment and evaluation of the ALJ reversal rate and simply required that the SSA review all of the ALJ decisions and report on that review. There was no mention in the amendment itself or the legislative history (but for the introductory statement of Senator Bellmon) that the SSA should focus on allowance decisions or target only ALJs with high allowance rates.

THE TRAGEDY OF THE DISABILITY AMENDMENTS OF 1980 AND THE BELLMON AMENDMENT

W hat followed the passage of the Bellmon Amendment was catastrophic.

To recap,[38] The second major provision of the Disability Amendments of 1980 called for periodic review of disability determinations (Section 311). Herein, Congress provided that all persons classified by SSA as being disabled ... would be subjected to review to prove continuing disability at least once every three years.

This cessation review process was to become effective on January 1, 1982. However, the SSA was eager to begin the deliberations (you need an early start to save $3.4 billion), and so the three-year review began in March 1981.

As of February 25, 1983, seven hundred forty-eight thousand cases of the once-judged disabled were reviewed, and benefits ceased

---

38   Ibid., 116.

in 45 percent of those cases. Out of total cases reviewed, seventy-four thousand, eight hundred involved claims of mental impairment with 42 percent of these beneficiaries being removed from the roles. As a result, *the caseload for ALJs rose 86.6 percent from 1979 to 1983,* placing a mammoth burden on an already languishing process.

From March 1981 to March 1983, ALJs restored benefits in 60 percent of all appeals and *reinstated (would you believe) 91 percent of mental cases....* The harshness and brutality of these cessations was compounded by a 1982 General Accounting Office report that indicated that *35 percent of those receiving benefits had shown little or no improvement in the medical conditions* that had originally made them eligible for benefits.

These mind-boggling statistics illustrate why SSA officials so desperately needed legislation that would ensure their actions be reviewed by compliant and subservient judges. They could not live with a corps of administrative law judges who reversed 91 percent of their "fair and impartial" decisions.

I was the administrative law judge in charge (ALJIC) of the Doraville, Georgia, hearing office from 1981 to 1987. Not only was our office flooded with hearing requests during that period of time, but most embarrassingly, our office and hearing offices throughout the country were besieged by the media. Newspapers regularly featured on their front pages photos of claimants in wheelchairs holding the notice from SSA that they were "not disabled."

The most egregious incident I personally was aware of occurred in a funeral home, where the deceased had died after receiving a notice that his disability benefits were to be terminated. The family was so visibly upset that they placed in the decedent's hands the notice stating that he was not disabled.

The above represents my very personal and parochial view from my small office in Georgia. In *Judges, Bureaucrats, and the Question of Independence: A Study of the Social Security Hearing Process,* Cofer provides a broader, national view:[39]

"While Margaret Heckler, the current HHS Secretary, boasted that there are fewer people on the disability rolls now than at any time since 1978, horror stories of the effects of cessation of disability benefits on individuals lives appeared in the news media in every section of the United States. Stories of persons committing suicide over the loss of benefits, persons reliant upon welfare assistance and food stamps while awaiting a hearing, and accounts of former claimants who died from the very medical condition(s) the SSA had determined not to be disabling filled the media. Workers, perceiving themselves victimized by the cessation hatchet, formed organizations through which to voice their alarm. Examples were the Alliance for Social Security Disability Recipients (Charlotte, North Carolina), Disabled American Workers Security (Denver, Colorado), and Stop Abuse of the Disabled (Boston, Massachusetts). Constituent pressures upon Congress became intense, and numerous hearings were held concerning the allegedly arbitrary nature of the denials."

Examples[40] of such accounts include "In the New Rush for Budget Savings, A Life is Trampled," *The Washington Post*, May 27, 1982; "I was denied Social Security Disability Dies of Illnesses," *The Los Angeles Times*, September 17, 1982; "Congress Considers Revising Review Procedures for Disability Payments to Aid the Beneficiaries," *The Wall Street Journal*, August 18, 1982; "She Lost Her Benefits, Her Will to Live," *Philadelphia Daily News*, June 10, 1982; "Fairness of Reagan's Cutoffs of Disability Aid Questioned," *The New York Times*,

---

39 Ibid., 117.
40 Ibid., 153.

May 9, 1982; "Social Security Harming Disabled, Critics Charge," *The Denver Post,* March 21, 1982; "When 'Fit for Work' Doesn't Fit," *Fort Lauderdale News/Sun Sentinel,* September 12, 1982; "Delays Frustrate Many in Disability Appeals," *Kansas City Star,* October 19, 1982.

The Social Security Administration had overplayed its hand.

Not only had SSA officials erroneously removed thousands of disabled from the disability roles, but in their ham-fisted fashion, they had established unrealistic goals or quotas for judges, attempted without success to remove administrative law judges from office for low production, and, in general, played havoc with significant provisions of the Administrative Procedures Act.

The tide was about to turn.

THE COURTS AND THE CONGRESS FINALLY TAKE CONTROL

~~~~~

S ocial Security Administration officials believed that they could get the attention of the "low-producing" ALJs by filing charges against a few of the lowest producers

On July 22, 1982, John L. Poore, the Director of Field Administration, forwarded to the Regional Chief ALJs updated Initiatives and Objectives for OHA. Initiative III, labeled "Enhance Image and Credibility of OHA," contained the following instructions:

1. Monitor ALJs on monthly basis to identify underachieving ALJs.
2. Establish procedures to initiate adverse actions against ALJs who abuse time and attendance.
3. Identify those ALJs who averaged twenty or fewer dispositions between September 1981 and April 15, 1982.

Based on the data received, three ALJs had charges filed against them before the Merit Systems Protection Board (MSPB):

- *Robert W. Goodman*, MSPB No. HQ75218210015
- *Jerry G. Brennan*, MSPB No. HQ75218210010
- *Stanley M. Balaban*, MSPB No. HQ75218210014

The OHA's single complaint against these ALJs was alleged inefficiency in the average number of cases they individually decided per month in a given time frame. No allegations of personal or judicial misconduct were made, nor of poor decisional quality. The OHA called for removal from office for "good cause."

Thus, productivity was the sole basis for requesting the firing of these three ALJs. In the 1980s, as an administrative law judge (ALJ) and the administrative law judge in charge (ALJIC) of a hearing office, I had more than a passing interest in these Draconian personnel actions. Further, Judge Goodman was stationed in Region IV, which had been part of my jurisdiction as the regional chief judge.

By way of background, I was both a very productive judge, averaging more than thirty-six cases per month, and also a high reversing judge, at more than 50 percent. I, of course, because of my high reversal rate, was a "targeted judge" under the provisions of the Bellmon Amendment because I did find favorably in a majority of the cases I had before me.

As a targeted judge, I did not feel threatened by the appellation, but, to the contrary, felt very secure that the quality and the correctness of my decisions made them impervious to any type of management attempt to change them using as their criteria budget and statistical data. My decisions were grounded solely on the evidence presented at the hearing and, in addition, I was able to incorporate in the framework and design of my decisions my early engineering training to first identify and define the issues that led to the appeal and then to use my legal knowledge and experience to prepare a suitable decision that would address those issues.

My thirty-plus years in the field of administrative law also served me in good stead. I took some pride in the fact that I required the presence of a vocational expert and, when available, a medical expert at each hearing. As noted earlier, a finding of disability must combine elements of medicine, knowledge of the workplace, and their symbiotic relationship with the law and the regulations. Having all three areas of expertise present at the claimant's hearing invariably leads to a decision that will be affirmed by the appellate courts if appealed.

The Social Security Administration, as expected, initially appealed a few of my favorable decisions pursuant to the 1980 Disability Amendments.

The attorneys for the claimants enjoyed sending me those appellate decisions restoring my favorable decisions, and I must admit that reading those decisions gave me great pleasure and delight.

For instance, in *Brown v. Heckler,* Civil Action No. C83-1874A US District Court, Northern District of Georgia, Atlanta Division, the appellate court ruled as follows:

In reversing the determination of the ALJ that plaintiff was disabled, the only rationale advanced by the Appeals Council was essentially, that the impairments documented by the medical evidence could not reasonably be expected to cause the type of pain and functional restriction which precludes sedentary work. There is no evidence in the medical record or elsewhere to support such an analysis. In making its own judgment, contradicted by the record, about the type of impairments that can cause disabling pain or functional restrictions, the Appeals Council has rendered a medical assessment which it is not qualified to make. This is an improper practice.

And in *Ray v. Heckler,* Civil Action No. C-83-90-G, US District Court, Northern District of Georgia, Gainesville Division, the court ruled as follows:

It is obvious that the ALJ found the plaintiff's testimony to be credible. Unless clearly erroneous, findings of fact, particularly those concerning credibility, are not be disturbed on appeal. This cavalier disregard for the findings of the ALJ is particular disturbing as it is unaccompanied by any elaboration of the reasons why the plaintiff's testimony is thought to be incredible, other than the recitation of an incorrect statement of law. The Secretary is ordered to reinstate the plaintiff's benefits and to reimburse her for the benefits which were wrongfully withheld as a result of the Secretary's erroneous decision.

The language of the court in *Smith v. Heckler,* Civil Action No. C83-26110A, US District Court, Northern District of Georgia, Atlanta Division, was especially heartwarming:

This case has a long and tortured history that the Court need not here relate. This case demonstrates just how far wrong this system can go. Smith has faced an interminable battle to acquire benefits to which he was clearly entitled. Indeed, the appeal process might well have been nearly as debilitating as Smith's other problems. The Court should have resolved or the parties should have resolved this matter long ago. The ALJ held that Smith was disabled. The ALJ was right. The Appeals Council was wrong.

For some inexplicable reasons, even though I was a high reversing judge, my favorable decisions no longer attracted the scrutiny of the Appeals Council for review and reversal.

But I digress; the attempt to dismiss three administrative law judges certainly did get the attention of the corps of ALJs. These personnel actions immediately raised a number of significant legal issues:

- Had the agency created a numerical quota in violation of the Administrative Procedures Act?
- Had the agency created a standard of performance in violation of the Administrative Procedures Act?
- Had the agency created a performance rating system in violation of the Administrative Procedures Act?
- Had the agency breached the terms of the Bono settlement?
- What criteria, if any, had been used to create a numerical standard that reflected the variety and difficulty of the cases assigned to a judge's docket?

Judge Goodman was located in a neighboring state, so I had some second-hand knowledge of his work ethic. He was one of the hardest working judges in the region. His decisions were of the highest quality. Unfortunately for him, the time and effort he spent on his decisions counted for naught with the agency. The bottom line was "numbers," and because of his legal scholarship in preparing a superior work product, his numbers suffered.

The Merit Systems Protection Board ruled that numbers of decisions issued by a judge could not be the sole basis for the dismissal of an ALJ. They recognized that without the presence of some reasonable standard that would take into account the difficulty of the cases assigned to a judge and other subjective criteria inherent in hearing a case, relying on numbers alone was not permissible. Such reliance was blatantly unfair. Since the Social Security Administration had failed to produce any valid statistical data that would define and delineate a reasonable national standard for ALJs that did not compromise their impartiality, SSA's petition to fire the three ALJs was dismissed.

On June 21, 1984, the reviewing of selected judges' cases was terminated. Why?

This decision to discontinue the review of cases under the Bellmon Amendment was probably based on a plethora of cases being decided in the federal courts nationwide. These cases uniformly held that the arbitrary reversal of favorable ALJ decisions by the Social Security Administration was in violation of the Administrative Procedures Act.

In *Hummel v. Heckler*, 736 F2nd 91 (3rd Cir. 1984) the US Circuit Court of Appeals ruled as follows:

It is, of course, axiomatic that trial before an unbiased judge is essential to due process. That due process rule is applicable to administrative as well as judicial adjudications. Indeed, the absence in the administrative process of procedural safeguards normally available in judicial proceedings has been recognized as a reason for even stricter application of the requirement that administrative adjudicators be impartial. Recognizing as much, the Social Security Administration has provided by regulation a means for raising a claim of bias before the agency.

The case was remanded for further proceedings consistent with this opinion.

Similarly in *Barry v. Bowen*, 825 F.2d 1324 (9nth Cir. 1987), the Ninth Circuit found that "when Bellmon Review was initiated, the SSA targeted for review those ALJs having an allowance rate of 66 2/3 percent or higher. By April 1983, the Bellmon Review Program had been expanded to target ALJs not only on the basis of their allowance rate but also on the basis of their Appeals Council Reversal Rate. The ALJ who heard Barry's case had been targeted for its own motion review, and when the ALJ granted Barry's claim, the decision was forwarded for review by the Appeals Council. The Appeals Council reversed, concluding that Barry was not entitled to disability benefits.

Barry sought review of this decision in the district court, claiming that the Review Program's targeting of certain ALJs had denied him due process. In defending against Barry's due process claim, the Secretary took essentially three positions: (1) that the district court could not hear plaintiff's constitutional claim because its jurisdiction is limited to an inquiry into whether the Appeals Council decision was supported by substantial evidence, (2) that a due process analysis was irrelevant so long as the Appeals Council decision was supported by substantial evidence, and (3) that Barry lacked standing because he had won his case before the ALJ.

"The district court rejected all of these arguments and found in Barry's favor in a carefully reasoned opinion. The district court noted that the Bellmon Review "put pressure on selected ALJs to reduce their percentage of benefit allowances, thereby denying claimants of their right to an impartial ALJ" and, in addition, sent a message that "impermissibly affected the Appeals council."

A serious issue as to whether the secretary acted in "bad faith" in denying a claim for disability benefits came before the Ninth Circuit in *Brown v. Sullivan*, 916 F.2d 492 (Ninth Circuit 1990). As in the cases cited above, an ALJ favorable ruling was appealed to the Appeals Council pursuant to the Bellmon Review Program. The Appeals Council modified the ALJ decision without reviewing the complete record, including a transcript of the administrative hearing. The district court found that the secretary's use of the Bellmon Review Program was a violation of Brown's due process rights and remanded the case to the ALJ to rule on the modifications made by the Appeals Council. Both parties requested that instead of a new hearing, the district court rule on the merits, rather than remanding the case. The district court agreed and reinstated the ALJ decision with none of the Appeals Council's modifications. The issue of attorneys' fees then arose. Ordinarily, by statute, attorney fees cannot exceed $75 per hour, but in cases involving "bad faith," which is defined as "vexatious, wanton, or oppressive conduct," attorney's fees are the "market rate," and in this case $125 per hour.

The Circuit Court of Appeals found that the Appeals Council's reversal of the ALJ decision without reviewing the entire record constituted bad faith and awarded attorney fees at the market rate of $125. In its decision, the Ninth Circuit stated, "We find that the cumulative effect of the Secretary's actions in the handling of Brown's case constitutes 'bad faith.'"

ASSOCIATION OF ADMINISTRATIVE LAW JUDGES, INC., V. HECKLER

‿

T he attempted firing of the three ALJs was to spur the Association of Administrative Law Judges to file suit in the US District Court to bar the Social Security Administration and the Department of Health and Human Services from continuing their unlawful interference in the adjudication of disability cases. Specifically, their announced initiative that punitive action would be taken against any ALJ who failed to meet arbitrary minimum numbers of case dispositions or failed to limit the number of favorable decisions he issued to disability claimants was in direct violation of the Administrative Procedures Act and cried out for injunctive relief.

As directed by the Board of Governors of the Association of Administrative Law Judges, Inc., Charles N. Bono, as president of the association, filed a lawsuit[41] challenging the Bellmon Review Program. The association was ably represented by Elliott L. Richardson, who had served as the secretary of the Department of Health, Education, and Welfare from 1970 to 1973. This is the same Elliott Richardson who ten

---

41 *Association of Administrative Law Judges, Inc. v. Heckler*, 594 F.Supp. 1132 Civil
    Action No, 83–0124, (US District Court, District of Columbia).

years earlier had awarded the prestigious Secretary's Special Citation to Dale Cook in recognition of his outstanding leadership to the corps of administrative law judges and as the managerial director of the Bureau of Hearings and Appeals.

The trial of these issues took place between February 28 and March 9, 1984, before District Court Judge Joyce Hens Green.

It was to be of considerable significance that after the trial, while the parties awaited a decision from Judge Green, the newly appointed associate commissioner (the former title was director) of the Office of Hearings and Appeals (as noted earlier) announced on June 21, 1984, that the practice of reviewing the cases of selected judges was terminated.

Up to this point, the validity of the Bellmon Review Program had been litigated only in collateral attacks by claimants who had been denied disability benefits. The association believed that to secure the decisional independence of its ALJs under the Administrative Procedures Act,[42] a direct challenge to the legislation was mandatory.

It is important to note for the record that it is not the decision of the ALJ that is appealed to the US District Court. The law governing ALJ decisions, *5 U.S.C §557(b)*, specifically provides that it is not the ALJ but the secretary of HHS who retains "all the powers which it would have in making the initial decision." Translated into everyday language, this means the following:

- If the decision of the ALJ is not appealed, it automatically becomes the decision of the secretary.
- Since ALJ decisions are subject to *sua sponte de novo* review by the Appeals Council, if the decision of the ALJ is appealed

---

42 Administrative Procedures Act (APA) 5 U.S.C. §551 et seq.

and reversed by the Appeals Council, then the Appeals Council decision becomes the decision of the secretary that can be appealed to the US District Court.

According to *Baker v. Heckler* 730 F.2d 1147, 1150 (8th Cir. 1984), "The statute authorizes the Secretary, not the ALJ, to make reviewable final decisions in disability cases."

Further, on matters of law and policy, the ALJs are entirely subject to the agency's regulations and pertinent statutes (*D'Amico v. Schweiker,* 698 F.2d 903, 907 [7th Cir. 1983]).

Therefore, the association, in its lawsuit, had to recognize that the decisional independence of the ALJ is a qualified independence.

The trial record and transcript makes reference to the "Hays Memorandum" dated September 24, 1982, which Judge Green,[43] in her decision, referenced as follows:

That memorandum explained the Bellmon Review was being instituted because of Congressional concern about high allowance rates and because only ALJ decisions denying benefits were generally subject to further review. Allowance rates were used as the basis for selecting the initial review group, in part, because studies had shown that decisions in this group would be the most likely to contain errors which would otherwise go uncorrected.

"Based upon own-motion rates individual ALJs were divided into four groups: 100 percent review; 75 percent review; 50 percent review; and 25 percent review.

---

43 *Association of Administrative Law Judges, Inc. v. Heckler.*

"Finally, the 'Hays Memorandum' advised that if, after further review, an ALJ's performance had not improved, 'other steps' would be considered. Understandably, plaintiff's members viewed that as a warning, OHA would recommend that charges be brought before the Merit Systems Protection Board (MSPB) seeking adverse personnel action, which could included dismissal."

In her decision, Judge Green made clear that OHA's reliance upon the Bellmon Amendment as commanding it to target high allowance ALJs for review was not supported by the congressional record, which chronicled the history of the legislation. In her decision, she found that "targeting high allowance ALJs for review … was of dubious legality for at least two reasons. First, that practice was not consistent with the language of the Bellmon Amendment nor its sparse legislative history … second, high allowance ALJs were initially targeted for review without regard to their actual own motion review rates in an overbroad sweep."

In any event, the Hays memorandum effectively framed the issue before the court that "the targeting of individual ALJs under Bellmon Review, based upon allowance rates and their own motion rates, was in essence an attempt to influence ALJs to reduce their allowance rates and thereby compromise their decisional independence."

And as stated in Plaintiff's Exhibit 110 (PX-110), "the Bellmon Review Program would result in illegal performance ratings of ALJs and would have the effect of chilling ALJ decisional independence."

And as stated in PX-17, "assuming no changed behavior on the part of the individual ALJ, Office of Appraisal would initiate a memorandum to the ALJ recommending that the ALJ file be turned over to the Office of Special Counsel for Administrative processing through OPM for appropriate action."

In support of its position, the association noted that "Mr. Hays sought advice from the Office of General Counsel for SSA, concerning the legality of targeting high allowance ALJs for Bellmon Review (Plaintiff's Exhibit-387). The office of General Counsel recognized that the Senate version of the Bellmon Amendment required such targeting but that the Conference Report did not. The Office of General Counsel inferred from the legislative history that targeting may have been perceived as having a possible chilling effect on the decisional independence of targeted ALJs. It concluded that while the law did not directly preclude targeting, there could be some legal risk, and suggested the desirability of reviewing some denial decisions."

"Although Mr. Hays had solicited the advice of the General Counsel, he did not accept it."

The alleged purpose of Bellmon review as expressed "by Mr. Hays emphatically at trial, has been that there is no agency policy to reduce allowance rates. The agency's policy is to reduce inconsistency in the application of law and regulations both within the ALJ corps and in the different levels of the adjudicatory process, and to reduce the number of decisions that do not correctly apply substantive agency policy. In keeping with this policy, OHA recognized that high allowance rates may indicate undue inconsistency of adjudicatory standards within SSA *[a backhanded reference to the continued use of POMS by SSA?]* and that a reduction of that inconsistency may result in or be reflected by some reduction in allowance rates among other things."

This "noble purpose" was substantially tarnished and discredited at trial when it was disclosed that "Mr. Hays had a financial interest to pressure the ALJs to reduce their allowance rates. As a member of the Senior Executive Service, he had a performance plan which stated as one of its goals or objectives the reduction of allowance rates. Mr.

Hayes performance was rated higher in FY 1981, a year in which such a reduction took place, than in FY 1982, when it did not. Significantly, Mr. Hayes had issued a memorandum to the ALJs, in which he said that ALJ allowance rates were 'untenable'" (Plaintiff's Exhibit 157).

In addition, testimony was received that representatives of the agency had stated to certain ALJs "that the only way to be free of OHA scrutiny was to lower their allowance rates to the national average of 45–55 percent." The named agency representatives disputed these allegations, stating that they had only "informed them of the national average" in response to their inquiry.

The most significant refutation of this noble purpose theory was that budgetary considerations motivated the targeting of ALJs. Plaintiff's Exhibit 29 stated that ALJs would be removed from Bellmon review when their allowance rates equaled or surpassed OHA's fiscal year goals.

In addressing OHA's position that its stated goal was to improve the quality accuracy of ALJ decisions, Judge Green found that "the evidence as a whole persuasively demonstrated that defendants retained an unjustifiable preoccupation with allowance rates, to the extent that ALJs could reasonably feel pressure to issue fewer allowance decisions in the name of accuracy. While there was no evidence that an ALJ consciously succumbed to such pressure, in close cases … that pressure may have intruded upon the fact finding process and may have influenced some outcomes.

"With reason plaintiff and its members viewed defendants' combined actions as a message to ALJs to tip the balance against claimants in close cases to avoid reversal or remand by the Appeals Council." It was common knowledge within the ALJ community that an increase in the numbers of their cases selected for review by the Appeals Council would result in their being placed on the Bellmon Review List.

At the trial, testimony was taken from an ALJ who testified that he felt compelled to practice defensive adjudication in order to protect himself and the record.

I personally can attest to the accuracy of that statement. As I have already noted, I was, because of my high allowance rates, on Bellmon Review, and since my last name started with the letter *B*, I had the added honor and distinction of heading the published ALJ Bellmon Review list when it was flashed on your television screen in connection with news stories dealing with aggrieved disability claimants.

I must admit that being on the Bellmon list improved both the quality and strength of my decisions. It was a real challenge, and as I signed my allowance decisions, I would silently say, "Let's see if you can find any basis to reverse this one!"

Based on the above recapitulation of the record, the reader, as I did, must conclude that a favorable decision from Judge Green was a foregone conclusion, *but ...*

As you may recall, while the parties awaited a decision from Judge Green, the newly appointed associate commissioner of the Office of Hearings and Appeals on June 21, 1984, terminated the Bellmon Program.

Judge Green, in her decision, noted the termination of this practice: "Perhaps in response to this litigation, defendants have modified the Bellmon Review Program significantly for the better," she wrote.

In her decision of September 10, 1984, Judge Green found the following:

"In sum, the Court concludes that defendants unremitting focus on allowance rates in the individual ALJ portion of the Bellmon Review Program created an untenable atmosphere of tension and unfairness which violated the spirit of the APA, if no specific provision thereof. Defendants insensitivity to that degree of decisional independence the APA affords to administrative law judges and the injudicious use of phrases such as 'targeting,' 'goals,' and 'behavior modification' could have tended to corrupt the ability of administrative law judges to exercise that independence in the vital cases that they decide."

Judge Green declined to grant the injunctive relief sought by the association, stating that "it would be unsuitable for the Court to order any affirmative relief under the present circumstances."

While the Corps of Administrative Law Judges was disappointed by Judge Green's denial of injunctive relief in the light of her conclusion that the agency had acted in violation of the APA, it should be noted that Judge Green also gave considerable weight to the following:

- That the agency's unilateral decision to terminate the Bellmon Review Program had sharply reduced any potential for conflict, and that the ALJs were now no longer subject to Bellmon Review obviated "the need for any injunctive relief"
- That the association, independent of any court intervention, had "achieved considerable success in its valid attempt to reveal and change agency practices"
- That the court had admonished SSA by stating that the agency would do well to consider whether any future

potential for the appearance of conflict might be avoided by some organizational modification

- The ingrained instinct of all courts to show deference to the agency authorized by statute to carry out a legislative and executive mandate. The judicial branch has no wish to micromanage a large administrative bureaucracy that it has neither the time, the training, nor the expertise to supervise.

"TIME TO REVIEW THE BIDDING," OR WHAT INSPIRED THE AMERICAN BAR ASSOCIATION TO COMMEND THE SOCIAL SECURITY ADMINISTRATIVE LAW JUDGES

~~~

The early 1980s were, in a real sense, preoccupied with conflicts in the executive, legislative, and judicial branches of our government regarding the extent that the rights of an individual dealing with a governmental agency can be circumscribed or limited by the agency for the sake of efficiency, productivity, or budgetary considerations.

Unhappily, the agency that was compelled by forces beyond its control, that is, legislation, budget cutbacks, economic downturns, and a host of other seemingly unrelated factors, to respond to a growing multitude of disabled persons seeking benefits under the aegis of the Social Security programs, was of course the Social Security Administration.

I have attempted in the foregoing to describe with specific incidents and statistical data what was occurring in the three branches of government in the late 1970s and early 1980s. Now, painting with a big brush, hopefully I can summarize in a coherent fashion what can best be described as to what was the status quo in 1986, the year of the ABA award.

At the Social Security Administration, there was and is an ongoing climate of tension and hostility between the agency and its administrative law judges. This tension between the need for efficiency, productivity, accountability, and decisional independence was present then, and, of course, continues to the present.

On the *legislative* front, it is clear from the above congressional history that the ALJs can declare "victory." The ALJs presented a strong and well-supported position that led Senators William S. Cohen and Carl Levin in their report dated September 16, 1983, to recommend the following:

1. The SSA immediately discontinue all Bellmon Review activity.
2. The SSA stop all managerial, administrative, and policy-related activity directly or indirectly aimed at influencing the ALJs' allowance rates.
3. The Judiciary Committees of the House and/or Senate review the propriety and legality of the SSA's actions regarding ALJ productivity.

On the *executive* front, we can call it a loss. As ALJs we came close to securing a seat in the upper echelons of the bureaucracy but were effectively thwarted when the seat we sought was reclassified as being in the competitive Civil Service and therefore not subject to executive appointment.

On the *judicial* front, I would call it a draw. The victories won by disabled plaintiffs in the courts, as noted below, generally dealt with the failure of SSA to document and support their attempted reversals of ALJ decisions. These were collateral attacks on the Bellmon Review Program that did not directly challenge the legality of the program. As the court found in *Ray v. Heckler*, Civil Action No. C-83-90-G, US District Court, Northern District of Georgia, Gainesville Division:

"It is obvious that the ALJ found the plaintiff's testimony to be credible. Unless clearly erroneous, findings of fact, particularly those concerning credibility, are not to be disturbed on appeal. This cavalier disregard for the findings of the ALJ is particularly disturbing as it is unaccompanied by any elaboration of the reasons why the plaintiff's testimony is thought to be incredible, other than the recitation of an incorrect statement of law."

And in *Brown v. Heckler,* Civil Action No. C83-1874A, US District Court, Northern District of Georgia, Atlanta Division, the court found that in making its own judgment, contradicted by the record, about the type of impairments that can cause disabling pain or functional restrictions, the Appeals Council has rendered a medical assessment which it is not qualified to make. This is an improper practice.

It was only *Association of Administrative Law Judges, Inc., v. Heckler,* 594 F.Supp. 1132 Civil Action No, 83-0124, US District Court, District of Columbia, that documented a direct confrontation between the ALJs and SSA. The judge did find that the Social Security Administration had violated the spirit of the Administrative Procedures Act, but failed to grant the injunctive relief requested by the Association of Administrative Law Judges.

However, the American Bar Association viewed our victories and losses in a much more favorable light than we as judges with the Social Security Administration had. From their detached and unbiased perspective, the American Bar Association realized that our unremitting, vigorous, and ultimately successful efforts to protect and defend the Administrative Procedures Act had protected the integrity of administrative adjudication within our agency, preserved the public's confidence in the fairness of governmental institutions, and upheld the rule of law; and as far as I know, this singling out and commending a specific group of administrative law judges was without precedent because ...

We had upheld the rule of law.

EPILOGUE

~

F lash forward twenty-three years to March 24, 2009, to a hearing before the Subcommittee on Income Security and Family Support of the House Committee on Ways and Means in the US House of Representatives.

It is disheartening to discover that over the past two decades, there has been no improvement in the administration of the Social Security's disability program. In fact, the situation has deteriorated.

Administrative Law Judge Ronald J. Bernoski, president of the Association of Administrative Law Judges, in his statement[44] and testimony dolefully described the status quo this way: "From SSA and AALJ, communication and cooperation are almost absent and both are needed."

In the early 1980s, the backlogs and ALJ productivity were the agency's primary concern with the disability program. In this new century, backlogs and ALJ productivity still dominate the agency's agenda.

---

44 Statement of Ronald J. Bernoski, as president of the Association of Administrative Law Judges before the Subcommittee on Social Security and Subcommittee on Income Security and Family Support of the House Committee on Ways and Means, March 24, 2009.

The backlog has risen and is now more than seven hundred fifty-six thousand disability cases. Sixty percent of this backlog, four hundred fifty-five thousand cases, are waiting in hearing offices to be prepared or "worked up" for a judge to review and hear.

Judge Bernoski, in his statement documents, that historically the backlog has always been the result of staff shortages at the administrative law judge level. When a case arrives at the hearing office, the case must be prepared for use in the hearing, which not only requires skill but at least one to three hours of time. This task is done by a senior case technician, who must select all pertinent exhibits and identify the source, eliminate duplications, arrange the exhibits in chronological order, and paginate, label, and prepare a list of all exhibits.

The current staffing levels are the lowest in decades.

Over the past twenty-three years, the SSA's initiatives to reduce the backlog have remained the same. SSA acknowledges the need for qualified personnel but regretfully still continues to rely on the failed initiatives of the 1980s—that providing more training, more guidelines, and more automation, such as electronic files, would resolve the backlog. The agency traditionally resists any efforts to redefine the concept of disability at the state agency level, preferring instead its own interpretation of legislative mandates.

The Fox study[45] echoes the Daub report,[46] Improving the Social Security Administration's Hearing Process, which concluded that "this growth in backlogs and in waiting times that would accompany it is not inevitable. There are three ways to avoid it.

---

45 Fox, "Observations on Disability Evaluation."
46 Improving the Social Security Administration's Hearing Process, Hal Daub, Chairman.

1. One is to increase the resources expended on the hearing process.
2. The second way to reduce backlogs is to reduce the flow of cases into the hearing process.
3. The third way to reduce backlogs is to increase production levels."

Judge Bernoski describes SSA's current house initiatives to reduce the backlog as "smoke and mirrors" and "silver bullet solutions."

The SSA continues to ignore the Daub[47] report in terms of increasing the resources available to the ALJs, and the staffing for ALJs is the lowest in decades. Daub opined that "SSA acknowledges the need for qualified personnel but not in sufficient numbers, believing that automation will replace experienced personnel. What has been and is still needed first is more staff to support the current judges."

The second recommendation of the Daub report, dealing with a reduction of the flow of cases to the ALJs, continues to be ignored by SSA. Yet, it is the eight-hundred-pound gorilla in the hearing process.

The Social Security Administration Summary of Performance for the fiscal year 2009 reports it completed 2.8 million disability applications.

If we apply the findings of the 2000 statistical data (40 percent of claims were allowed at the state agency level, another 4 percent were allowed at the reconsideration level, 38 percent were denied by the state agency but did not pursue their claim to the hearing level, and the remaining 18 percent did pursue their claim to the hearing level)[48]

---

47 Ibid.
48 Ibid.

to the number of disability claims filed in the year 2009, rounding the numbers, we can extrapolate the following:

- Total number of cases in the pool—2,800,000—100 percent
- Cases paid by state agency—1,232,000—44 percent
- Cases appealed to ALJs—504,000—18 percent
- Cases not appealed to ALJ level—1,064,000—38 percent

The performance report for fiscal year 2009 states that 622,851 requests for hearing were received, approximately 22 percent of the total filings. Thus, in terms of requests for a hearing before an ALJ between the years 2000 and 2009, we have roughly a range of between 18 percent and 22 percent.

If we assume, based *on the year 2000 data,* that if approximately 20 percent of the denied disability claimants, or 100,800 people (20 percent x 504,000 = 100,800), were in fact to be found disabled by the state agency by ignoring the POMS, the number of cases appealed to the ALJ level would drop from the 504,000 figure to 403,200 cases (504,000 – 100,800 = 403,200).

If we assume based *on the year 2009 data* that if approximately 20 percent of the denied disability claimants, or 123,200 (20 percent x 616,000 = 123,200), were, in fact, to be found disabled by the state agency by ignoring the POMS, the number of cases appealed to the ALJ level would drop from the 616,000 figure to 492,880 cases (616,000 – 123,200 = 492,800).

By the elimination of between 100,000 and 125,000 cases annually from the ALJ hearings level, one could assume that the backlog would quickly disappear.

The use of the 20 percent figure, which admittedly is quite arbitrary, is in fact a very conservative assumption based on the administrative law judges' historical reversal rates of between 60 and 80 percent.

In terms of cost, it would essentially be a wash, since the disabled applicant would be entitled to the same benefits, but a year earlier, by being found disabled at the state agency level, rather than at the ALJ hearing level.

The third recommendation of the Daub report to eliminate the backlog was to increase the productivity of the ALJs. If the Social Security Administration continues its current office configurations, increasing productivity will be difficult, if not impossible. As the reader may recall, the Social Security Administration in the early 1980s, because of its ongoing obsession with reversal rates, radically modified the chain of command structure in the hearing office when it institutionalized the "Model Hearing Office" concept.

Historically, the hearing office chief administrative law judge (HOCALJ) was the key figure responsible for maintaining and improving the performance of the hearing office. Having served as a HOCALJ for almost fifteen years, I must admit it is a labor of love, with multiple responsibilities and few rewards.

As the HOCALJ, you are responsible for the overall management and effectiveness of the hearing office, have administrative and managerial responsibility for all support staff in the hearing office, and are to provide leadership and administrative direction to the ALJs as may be required in the course of general office management. In addition to all of these duties, the HOCALJ is responsible for a full docket of cases, holding hearings and issuing decisions. The Civil Service official description of the position lists two pages of duties and responsibilities.

The individual ALJ in the past was in charge of a "unit" that was composed of a senior case technician, a secretary, and a staff attorney. Once a case was received in the hearing office, it was immediately assigned to one of the ALJ units. This was a team effort, and each unit strove to make sure that its team compared favorably with the other office teams. The ALJ as the team leader had direct control over his staff in terms of assigned duties, goals, and the most powerful tool of all, the job performance annual rating. The HOCALJ and his administrative staff were available to the ALJ if the ALJ requested extra assistance or had personnel problems. The system worked well, and in fact, it was the ALJ's staff that took special pride in their unit to be sure it was "numero uno" in the office.

As noted above, in order to gain some modicum of control over the independence, productivity, and reversal ratios of the ALJs, the Social Security Administration in the 1980s, in the guise of assisting the ALJs to devote more time to hearing cases and less time to administrative chores, removed all ALJ control, direction, and responsibility over:

- selecting pertinent exhibits in the case,
- preparing an exhibit list,
- scheduling cases for hearing,
- monitoring the hearing at the hearing office or at a remote hearing site, and
- ensuring that an appropriate recording of the hearing was made.

All of these duties, responsibilities and, most important, staff to carry them out were transferred to a hearing office director (HOD), whose sole responsibility was to ensure that when the ALJ entered the hearing room, a fully prepared case file was at "the bench." Certainly, the HODs do their best to be sure that the ALJ has a quality product, but if, as might be expected, on occasion there are deficiencies in the case file, the ALJ is totally responsible for any deficiencies in the record, even though he had no input in the process that produced the deficiency.

This management technique totally isolated the ALJs from the hearing office and its personnel, and in this setting it is obvious that, as stated in third recommendation of the "Daub Report," any effort by an individual ALJ to increase productivity is successfully sabotaged and stymied.

This dichotomy at the hearing office, where the management portion of the office has productivity goals that in the past, when implemented, threatened the decisional independence of the administrative law judge, is a recipe for disaster for both the Social Security Administration and its ALJs. This inevitable tension, between the hearing office managers and the HOCALJ and ALJs, is a ticking time bomb.

Thus, again, we have the classic battle between the agency's desire to gain control over the independence and productivity of the ALJs by the use of its permissible management initiatives, and the ALJs' resistance to any initiatives that threaten their judicial independence and the need to uphold the rule of law.

Scholars over the last forty years have struggled, without success, to find a solution to this classic confrontation. As requests for a disability hearing continue unabated, and since all parties agree that delays of a year or two are indefensible, it would appear that the only workable solution that would not result in a massive hemorrhaging of benefits would be to adopt the first recommendation of the Daub Report, which proposed a massive infusion of resources to the Office of Hearings and Appeals, now the Office of Disability and Review (ODAR).

A quarter of a century later, we find ourselves back at square one. The Social Security Administration, for budgetary reasons, finds it politically and financially impossible to change its disability procedures at the state agency level. And the administrative law judges following the rule of law will continue to reverse 70 to 80 percent of those appealed decisions with the approval of the US Supreme Court,[49] which concluded that the fact that the Social Security ALJs decide against the government in about half the disability cases they hear "attests to the fairness of the system and refutes any implication of impropriety."

As stated in the Daub Report, if "in the last several years Congress had given the Social Security Administration the $720 million that the president requested, which equates to about nine thousand work years, there would have been no backlogs in the hearing offices."

It can reasonably be expected that in the foreseeable future, there will be a massive infusion of financial resources directed at eliminating the backlog, and if correctly and effectively expended, that will, as noted in the Daub Report, eliminate the backlog problem.

A word of caution! The Social Security Administration has a long history of interference in the functioning of its administrative law judges. Wiser heads in the Social Security Administration must see the need to change its relationship with its ALJs from one of confrontation to cooperation. There is a massive residue of mistrust that goes back at least as far as the late 1970s, when pressures to reduce the numbers of allowances and increase the number of decisions led to a situation that was described as "an agency at war with itself."

As noted earlier, in the 1970s and 1980s, the Social Security Administration, for political reasons, embarked on a review of favorable

---

49 *Richardson v. Perales*, 402 U.S. 389 (1971).

decisions by administrative law judges. Under the guise of the Bellmon review, it designed a program to encourage judges to be sure that their decisions would comport well with the POMS manual rather that the Social Security law.

A good deal of this mistrust is a result of the Social Security Administration's misuse of its recognized authority to provide legitimate management techniques to process the ALJ caseload more efficiently. The Social Security Administration must recognize that the legislative and judicial branches of this government will not permit it to again unilaterally create initiatives that fail to recognize that ALJ reversal rates are valid and comport well with the Administrative Procedures Act. A good start might be to roll out a pilot program that would incorporate the proposals[50] that I submitted as president of the Association of Administrative Law Judges on July 11, 1973, to the US Civil Service Commission.

The five proposals I submitted thirty-seven years ago are as follows:

1. The administrative law judges must be given the authority to remand cases to the Bureau of Disability Insurance.
2. The appeal of a denied claim must be filed within sixty days.
3. Before a claim is denied by the state agency, the denied claimant must be provided a personal interview.
4. That adversary hearings be required in problem cases where the ability of the administrative law judge to cross-examine the claimant is limited because it might reflect some animus toward the claimant.

---

50 Statement of Frank B Borowiec, Administrative Law Judge, President of the Association of Administrative Law Judges in the Department of Health, Education and Welfare presented to the Advisory Committee on Utilization of Administrative Law Judges, Civil Service Commission, on July 11, 1973.

5. The same review standards must be adopted at the state agency and administrative law judge levels.

Strangely, thirty-seven years later, these proposals still have a certain freshness and appeal.

And as a gesture of good faith, the Social Security Administration could remove the current isolation of the administrative law judge from the hearing office and its personnel by replacing the current "pool system" with the "unit system," which historically inspired pride in the work product, improved morale, and enhanced productivity. The current pool system calls to mind an old adage:

When everyone is responsible to somebody,
Then no one is responsible to anybody.

In any event, a new generation of administrative law judges in the Social Security Administration will be called upon

To protect
the integrity of administrative adjudication within their agency, to preserve the public's confidence in the fairness of governmental institutions, and to uphold the Rule of Law.